NEW DIRECTIONS FOR CHILD DEVELOPMENT

William Damon, *Brown University*
EDITOR-IN-CHIEF

Religious Development in Childhood and Adolescence

Fritz K. Oser
University of Fribourg

W. George Scarlett
Tufts University

EDITORS

Number 52, Summer 1991

JOSSEY-BASS INC., PUBLISHERS, San Francisco

MAXWELL MACMILLAN INTERNATIONAL PUBLISHING GROUP
New York • Oxford • Singapore • Sydney • Toronto

RELIGIOUS DEVELOPMENT IN CHILDHOOD AND ADOLESCENCE
Fritz K. Oser, W. George Scarlett (eds.)
New Directions for Child Development, no. 52
William Damon, Editor-in-Chief

Microfilm copies of issues and articles are available in 16mm and 35mm,
as well as microfiche in 105mm, through University Microfilms Inc., 300
North Zeeb Road, Ann Arbor, Michigan 48106.

LC 85-644581   ISSN 0195-2269   ISBN 1-55542-788-X

NEW DIRECTIONS FOR CHILD DEVELOPMENT is part of The Jossey-Bass
Education Series and is published quarterly by Jossey-Bass Inc., Publishers, 350 Sansome Street, San Francisco, California 94104-1310 (publication number USPS 494-090). Second-class postage paid at San Francisco,
California, and at additional mailing offices. POSTMASTER: Send address
changes to New Directions for Child Development, Jossey-Bass Inc.,
Publishers, 350 Sansome Street, San Francisco, California 94104-1310.

SUBSCRIPTIONS for 1991 cost $48.00 for individuals and $70.00 for institutions, agencies, and libraries.

EDITORIAL CORRESPONDENCE should be sent to the Editor-in-Chief,
William Damon, Department of Education, Box 1938, Brown University,
Providence, Rhode Island 02912.

Cover photograph by Wernher Krutein/PHOTOVAULT © 1990.

Printed on acid-free paper in the United States of America.

CONTENTS

EDITORS' NOTES

Everyone knows there are differences between the religiosity of children, youth, and adults. We need no reminder that growing older can bring profound and diverse changes in the way individuals pray, talk about God, and worship. Equally obvious is the fact that the public face of adult religion shows a many-colored robe—from the Shabbat meal of a Jewish family to the solemn Mass of Roman Catholics, from the silent meetings of Quakers to the Friday pray of Moslems, from Buddhist offerings to the worship of Indian Goddesses. And while difference in ritual is what strikes the eye, even greater difference is heard by the ear. We listen to myths about the origins of the world as fantastic as any science fiction book, and then we turn to tightly reasoned arguments from theologians nurtured on modern philosophy.

The diversity we experience in religion goes much further than age changes and differences in public religion. Within the same institutional religion, we find some with a stern and punitive God, others talking freely to God as they would to a friend, and still others groping as if in a fog trying to make contact with someone that only might be "out there"; we find some praying for God to take control, others praying for strength to carry out life's tasks, and others not praying at all. We see, then, diversity in private as well as in public religion.

What is the common core in all this diversity? Is there a basic "mother structure" of religious feeling and thinking that binds the diversity we find across ages and across different expressions of public and private religion? This volume, *Religious Development in Childhood and Adolescence,* addresses these questions from the developmental perspectives of different theories. More specifically, the volume is about the development of private religion and the inner dynamic that pushes children, youth, and adults to construct and reform their views and change their feelings as they mature and adapt to life's new problems.

How do we describe and explain development? How do we reconcile scientific models of religious development with the notion of religion as eternal truth? And what place does a developmental perspective on religion have for those who feel no connection to a God or Ultimate Being, who lack "faith"? These questions, too, are addressed here.

But the main goals of this volume are broader than those implied by these questions. By taking a developmental perspective, we hope to show that religion is not a frozen set of rituals and beliefs but rather an ever-changing, dynamic force with its own logic and purpose. We hope, too, that by being faithful to religion as experienced, we can help the theologian meet the demands that arise when faith seeks understanding. And, finally, we hope to demonstrate the usefulness of a developmental perspective in explaining the diversity that is religion. The volume is divided into two parts. The three chapters of Part One present very general perspectives on religious development. In Chapters One and Two, Oser and Fowler provide stage approaches to religious judgment and faith, respectively. Both have been influenced by cognitive-developmental psychology, but not to the point of reducing religion to general cognitive processes operating on religious content. Readers familiar with theology as well as psychology will detect in these chapters the themes of Paul Tillich and H. Richard Niebuhr as much as those of Jean Piaget and Lawrence Kohlberg. In contrast, in Chapter Three, Rizzuto provides an object relations perspective on religious experience, showing in what ways religious experiences and representations of God lend themselves to conceal and reveal experiences with significant objects from the past and present. But unlike Freud's relatively static view of religion, Rizzuto sees the transformation of God and object representations as a potential means for the modulation of universal human tensions (for example, between dependence and autonomy, loving and being loved).

The chapters of Part Two discuss specific topics and past research in religious development. The first three chapters of Part Two remind us of what an active time adolescence can be for religious development. In Chapter Four, Scarlett and Perriello focus on the functions of prayer that only first appear in adolescence and that make prayer in adolescence structurally quite different from prayer in childhood. In Chapter Five, Reich details the development of complementarity reasoning in adolescence: a new way of thinking to resolve the many (apparent) contradictions permeating religion. In Chapter Six, Nipkow and Schweitzer explain religious doubt in late adolescence in terms of failed expectations: expectations of God and particularly of organized religion. In Chapter Seven, Bucher offers a structural explanation for age changes in children's understanding of parables (and of Scripture in general). Finally, in Chapter Eight, Bucher and Reich's annotated bibliography reminds us that there is much work to be done. Their bibliography shows how and why there has been so little written on religious development, which is another justification for this volume.

W. George Scarlett
Fritz K. Oser
Editors

W. George Scarlett is assistant professor of child study in the Eliot-Pearson Department of Child Study, Tufts University, Medford, Massachusetts.

Fritz K. Oser is professor of educational psychology and chair at the Pedagogical Institute, University of Fribourg, Fribourg, Switzerland.

PART ONE

General Perspectives on Religious Development

Religious judgment is the way in which an individual reconstructs his or her experience from the point of view of a personal relationship with an Ultimate (God). Religious development is concerned with the age-related, meaning-making qualities of this reconstruction.

The Development of Religious Judgment

Fritz K. Oser

The Developmental Frame in the Study of Religious Judgment

Religion as experienced, institutional religion, and religion as defined by theologians and philosophers differ considerably from one another. In this chapter, I focus on the first sense of religion: questions of how individuals experience religion and use religion to create meaning and find direction. My answers to these questions are framed in terms of the development of religious judgment and what underlies that development, namely, transformations in the way individuals define their relationships to God or some Ultimate Being in concrete situations. (The term God or Gods refers to one or more personalized Ultimate Beings and is related to the revelations of particular religions, whereas the term Ultimate Being refers to a less narrow description of a divine being to which an individual feels committed. In this chapter, both terms are used interchangeably. The term Divine Reality would be the least precise notion.)

Only a few efforts have attempted to address the issues of religious experience and meaning making (for an overview, see Meadow and Kahoe, 1984). For example, there have been applications of the Piagetian model of logical development to religious contents (Elkind, 1964a, 1964b, 1970, 1971; Goldman, 1964), attempts to conceptualize religious development as a combination of self, morality, logic, and meaning-making processes (Fowler, 1974, 1976, 1981, this volume; Power, 1988), and studies aimed at understanding

I thank Wolfgang Althof, Anton A. Bucher, K. Helmut Reich, and W. George Scarlett for their suggestions, constructive critiques, and translational help.

the development of ontological categories (Broughton, 1978, 1980a, 1980b; Fetz, 1982, 1985). Apart from these approaches, there have been few investigations directed at building up a theory about the development of an individual's constructions and reconstructions of religious experiences and beliefs. For this reason, many of us in the field of religious development are attempting to formulate a new paradigm of religious development, using a structural concept of discontinuous, stagelike development and the classical semiclinical interview method as our primary research strategy.

What do we mean by religious judgment? We do not mean judgment based simply on dogmas or religious traditions. Nor do we mean judgment based on any content or descriptive notion such as "God is almighty." Rather, we mean reasoning that relates reality as experienced to something beyond reality and that serves to provide meaning and direction beyond learned content. Such reasoning may occur at any time but is especially likely in times of crisis, as in the following example:

> A boy from a junior high school suffered a serious motorcycle accident that left him with a broken spine and the loss of any ability to walk. His classmates asked their teacher to help them sort out questions arising from the accident, in particular, the question of how God could have let this happen. Some spoke of chance, not God, governing destiny. Others argued that God still governs but in ways that are often unfathomable. For awhile the teacher did not intervene. Then, after several students expressed fear of losing their faith, the teacher shared his belief that a strong faith can only emerge when engaging the world as it really is: full of conflict, injustice, sickness, and death.

What happened in this situation? The students were forced to rethink their individual relationships to God because those relationships provided them with a crucial means to make sense of a particular tragedy. In short, their assessment of the accident involved religious judgments made in the light of their conceptions of how God and they are related. In other words, they interpreted a contingency situation by engaging their religious deep structures of reflection. These "contingency" situations, or at least perceived contingency situations, constitute, in Aristotelian terminology, a fact, a state of affairs, or a process that does not exist or happen necessarily or logically. It could also be in the opposite direction or not at all; there does not exist any rational argument for why it is as it is and is not in some other way. But not only contingency situations call for religious judgment. Sometimes situations are such that individuals are deeply touched by a particular event or are led to reflect on general goals in their lives. These deep structures inform their religious knowledge, their religious attachment, and their religious feelings. Religious judgments represent a form or quality of acts of balancing different value elements against each other, struggling for faith, rehearsing and rejecting solutions, and building up religious "views" of the world's ontological and cultural unevenness.

This example also illustrates how religious judgment is a construction and capacity that can change and develop with age. In the students' collective judgment there was a disequilibrium, a sense of something being out of balance. But this was not the case in what the teacher had to say. A developmental theory of religious judgment thus states that, as in the prior example, an individual relates his or her experience to an Ultimate Being (God), and that this is done *in qualitatively different ways during the life cycle, depending on the developmental stage.* In concrete situations, this connection is expressed through religious discourse and prayer, religious interpretation of events, religious texts and signs, and participation in religious or religiously conceived ceremonies. The individual's understanding of all these activities is filtered and shaped by his or her given stage structure, which is more or less intense or explicit, more or less autonomous, more or less balanced as far as religious expression is concerned, and more or less reversible with respect to the criteria discussed shortly here.

How can we describe this reconstructive religious capacity more thoroughly? How can we identify qualitatively different forms of religious reasoning that are developmentally connected to one another? From a first set of data resulting from interviews with individuals of different ages about their religious meaning making, my colleagues and I extracted seven polar dimensions that emerged in all of the interviews. Moreover, we found similar dimensions when consulting the most important studies on the nature of religion, such as those of Eliade (1957) and Durkheim (1915), and when reviewing the history of theology.

As discussed shortly, we used these seven dimensions to construct religious dilemmas and the respective probe questions for interview purposes. We found that an individual must balance these dimensions and relate them to each other in order to render the religious construction of a particular life situation, or, in other words, to produce a religious judgment.

The first polar dimension is *freedom versus dependence.* An individual's feeling of having been cast into this world and the experience of his or her natural limits are often rationalized by a notion of dependence on the Ultimate Being's decision making. Persons ask themselves to which extent God (the Ultimate Being) might let them have their own way and to which extent obedience is demanded. Religious judgment typically shows an awareness of both dependence and freedom (with respect of God's will), but developmental differences are marked when analyzed for stage characteristics. At a lower stage, in religiously significant situations, individuals tend to see the dependence as immediate; and conversely, they also see individual freedom as given directly by the Ultimate Being. The higher the stage, the more both types of experience are seen as mutually determined (and mutually dependent): Freedom is achieved via experiences of dependence, and we are dependent because we know that it is the connection to God that gives us freedom. Thus, the "will of God" is internally related to the free will of human beings. The second polar dimension is *transcendence versus immanence*. Again, at the lower stages of development, one pole is in focus to the exclusion of the other, or the two poles are experienced as opposites: either God intervenes directly or he does not, either he is inside or outside of our world. At higher stages, transcendence is experienced as emerging indirectly, through a person's good actions, style, listening, interpreting, and commitments to the welfare of others, so that eventually immanence becomes a necessary priority for transcendence, and vice versa.

The third polar dimension is *hope versus absurdity*. At first, situations determine whether or not an individual feels hope; questions about whether life is absurd or full of hope simply do not exist. But with development come such questions, which are initially answered by pitting one pole against the other. Eventually, the two are understood in terms of each other: Hope supersedes absurdity, but the experience of absurdity remains a necessary (though not sufficient) condition for hope.

The fourth polar dimension is functional *transparency versus opacity*. This dimension refers to how individuals understand God's will, how they judge or read the "signs." At lower stages, either pole is acceptable in particular situations. With development, one pole is acceptable in particular situations, and one pole is accepted over the other: Either an event reveals God's will and action or God's will remains inscrutable. At the highest stages, individuals create a tension between what seems a "sign" (transparency) coming from what is essentially mysterious. We see, but "through a glass darkly."

The fifth polar dimension is *faith (trust) versus fear (mistrust)*. The message may be "Trust in the Lord" while the primary experience is fear and loneliness in face of sickness, suffering, and death. At lower stages, these poles are unequilibrated: Faith does not allow for fear, nor fear for faith. With development, however, strong faith, or deeply felt trust, comes especially through having feared, through coping with life's vicissitudes and "dark nights of the soul."

The sixth and seventh polar dimensions are *the holy versus the profane* and *eternity versus ephemerity*, respectively. Again, at lower stages of development, individuals focus on only one pole while rejecting or ignoring the other. And at intermediate stages, the poles are understood as highly separate and exclusive, for example, feeling we have to abandon any idea of holiness in the world once we confront its profanity. At higher stages, the holy and eternity are seen in the most profane and ephemeral events or actions.

It is how these polar elements are coordinated that constitutes a person's religious deep structure. It is this deep structure that explains how individuals judge particular events, sermons, and religious texts. And it is the development of religious deep structure that constitutes the focus of the theory of religious judgment articulated in this chapter.

Measuring the Development of Religious Judgment

A religious judgment is made consciously; in contrast, an individual is usually unaware of the deep structure on which it is based. So, measurement and evaluation of a religious judgment require an interpretation of what it reveals about the underlying structure. But before discussing the way my colleagues and I interpreted judgments in order to reveal underlying structure, I need to say something about how we find out about such judgments in the first place.

Religious Dilemmas. Religious judgments occur spontaneously in a variety of situations: in prayer, meditation, religious celebration, and crisis. But these situations are difficult to study for a variety of reasons, especially ethical ones. So, my research group followed the Piaget-Kohlberg research paradigm and elicited religious judgments from hypothetical dilemmas dealing with religiously significant problems of a reasonably universal nature.

The most widely used dilemma describes a situation in which Paul, a young medical doctor, sits in a plane about to crash. Out of desperation, he promises to dedicate his life to the sick and poor in Third World countries if he survives the crash. He does survive and then struggles with whether or not to keep his promise. A second dilemma describes a situation similar to Job's: A judge who has led a good and responsible life finds himself in misery and pain, asking why a just man has to suffer so much. This dilemma poses questions about God's justice, will, and power. And a third dilemma deals with whether certain events (for example, winning the lottery) occur solely by chance or whether they can be attributed to a divine plan. These three dilemmas were selected out of a total of twelve because they, more than the others, evoked strong reactions and because they could be understood by individuals from a variety of cultures and religious traditions (with, of course, some changes made in content as we went from one culture to another).

In semiclinical interviews, our subjects were asked what they would do if they were the actors in the stories, and why. Responses to these questions and follow-up questions revealed the subjects' religious deep structures and demonstrated that the structure of religious thought is independent of its content.

Stages of Religious Judgment. On the basis of extensive empirical study using these dilemmas to elicit religious judgments, we have been able to discern five qualitatively different forms of religious judgment. In the process of theory building, that is, of identifying major features of possible developmental stages, we followed the approach of interlinking and mutual bootstrapping between theory and empirical investigation. A helix led from initial data to an intuitive theoretical model, then back to the data in order to modify and extend the model, and so on. The five stages defined below form a sequence. The model satisfies the criteria for a developmental theory as usually employed in the cognitive-developmental paradigm: (1) The stages of religious judgment are defined by operational structures differing not only in quantitative respects (number of elements) but also in qualitative respects (organization of elements). (2) The stages form structured wholes. (3) Their sequence follows an invariant developmental logic (empirically, no skipping of stages). (4) The sequence follows the law of hierarchical integration of the elements (the relations between the elements at a former stage become transformed and better integrated at the next higher stage). I introduce each stage with a brief synopsis (Table 1) before giving more details. But a sufficiently detailed description of the stages would require more space than is available here. The following outline thus presents only the most important features of each stage.

At *Stage 1*, the Ultimate Being is conceived as all-powerful, intervening directly in the world and in individuals' fates. The Ultimate Being is pro-

Table 1. Stages of Religious Judgment

Stage	Description
Stage 1	Orientation of religious heteronomy (*deus ex machina*). God (the Ultimate Being) is understood as active, intervening unexpectedly in the world. The human being is conceived as reactive; he or she is guided because the Ultimate Being is provided with power, with the possibility to make things happen.
Stage 2	Orientation of *do et des*, 'give so that you may receive.' God (the Ultimate Being) is still viewed as being always external and as an all-powerful being who may either punish or reward. However, the Ultimate Being can be influenced by good deeds, promises, and vows. The human being can exert a prophylactic influence (restricted autonomy, first form of rationalization).
Stage 3	Orientation of ego autonomy and one sided self-responsibility (deism). The influence of the Ultimate Being is consciously reduced. Transcendence and immanence are separated from one another. The human being is solipsistically autonomous, responsible for his or her own life and for secular matters. The Ultimate Being, if its existence is accepted, has its own domain of hidden responsibility.
Stage 4	Mediated autonomy and salvation plan. God (the Ultimate Being) is mediated with the immanence, as a cipher of the "self" per se. Multiple forms of religiosity are apparent, all accepting a divine plan that brings things to a good end. Social engagement becomes a religious form of life.
Stage 5	Orientation to religious intersubjectivity and autonomy, universal and unconditional religiosity. The individual's religious reasoning displays a complete and equilibrated coordination of the seven polar dimensions. Religion is more a working model than a security concept. The person feels that he or she has always been unconditionally related to the Ultimate Being: *unio mystica, boddhi,* and similar impressions.

vided with absolute power; it may protect or destroy, send something hurtful or joyful, dispense health or sickness. Often, it is assumed that God made all things, even mountains or big buildings, and caused all events, such as plane crashes. In addition to this artificialism (interpreting the origin of things as a concrete fabrication by an all-powerful divine being), children at this stage often show an anthropomorphic representation of God. The Ultimate Being's will must always and unreservedly be fulfilled; if not, the relationship breaks, and the Ultimate Being inflicts sanctions on the disobedient person. On the other hand, the individual's opportunities to influence the Ultimate Being are viewed as minimal. In the religious judgment interviews, this line of reasoning showed up when subjects stated, in response to the plane crash dilemma, that Paul has to fulfill his promise to God in order to avoid punishment, such as an accident or a stomach ulcer, directly sent by God.

At *Stage 2,* a major structural transformation is evidenced in a dramatic change regarding the conception of the relationship between the individual and the Ultimate Being. This stage can best be characterized by the Latin saying *do et des,* 'give so that you may receive,' just as the Romans sacrificed to the God of the winds in order to survive journeys on the Mediterranean Sea. At this stage, the individual is convinced that God's will and mood can be influenced by prayers, by good deeds, and by adherence to religious rules and customs. If one cares about the Ultimate Being and passes the tests it sends, the Ultimate Being will act like a trusting and loving father or mother, and the individual will be happy, healthy, and successful. In the Paul dilemma interview, subjects at this stage argued that Paul has to go to the Third World because God has done something good for him. If Paul refused to keep his promise, God would become angry and refuse to help him in the next situation of danger. Likewise, it could be reasoned (opposite content of choice but same structure) that Paul does not have to leave his hometown if he is willing to do a lot of good deeds for the poor and the sick, and if he gives a lot of money to relief organizations engaged in the Third World.

But what is going to happen if such good behavior is not rewarded, if the just person must suffer while the Ultimate Being does not lift a finger and wraps itself in silence? In the long run, such experiences are not compatible with the main orientation of Stage 2. The deep structure of religious reasoning has to be broken and transformed in order to cope with situations that do not fit the "tit-for-tat" view of the relationship. Henceforth, the individual feels responsible for his or her own life and destiny.

At *Stage 3,* reasoning can be characterized as "deistic" because the Ultimate Being is conceived as being apart from and outside of the world. The idea of a God in charge of all the details of human existence and nature is abandoned. Rather, it is assumed that God has a particular realm of action. In individual and social matters, an individual's will is crucial;

God's will cannot be known or is not directed to secular matters. This form of religious consciousness is widespread, particularly among adolescents. Evidently, there is a broader developmental foundation for an attitude claiming the separation of domains. Adolescents are in search of their identity; they demand ego autonomy, and often they rebel against external control, objecting to dependence on their parents as well as to the authority of religious institutions with their "antiquated" notions of life style and proper religiosity. The following statements regarding Paul's dilemma are characteristic of this stage: "Paul has to decide alone; I can't see God's will in his fate; all depends on his own will."

It is not surprising that we often find atheistic attitudes at this stage of development. Most of the time, they are explained by the subjects themselves as being caused by disillusionment: "God didn't help in situations of pain and anxiety; he didn't show up when I begged entreatingly. He tolerates unspeakable misery and injustice in the world. Obviously, he does not exist at all." However, we often find an attitude representing the opposite content, namely, an attitude in which autonomy of the self is abandoned, and God is viewed as the only authority to be "served." Examples of this attitude are the so-called youth religions or "cults." Thus, Stage 3 shows a particular imbalance of two autonomous realms, the immanent and the transcendent.

From having tested autonomy (or rejection of autonomy), individuals may come to a new realization about both the necessity and the limits of autonomy. At *Stage 4,* individuals recognize that their freedom and lives cannot originate and give meaning solely within themselves. Rather, in a global sense freedom and life have been made possible and meaningful through an Ultimate Being. Henceforth, God or the Ultimate Being is considered the bearing ground of the world and of each individual's existence. Now, an indirect, mediated relationship with God emerges. Individuals see themselves as free and responsible, but freedom now is tied to the Ultimate Being who gives and sustains freedom. Individuals at this stage often speak of a divine plan underlying and giving meaning to life's events, life's ups and downs. In the Paul dilemma, persons at this stage typically answer that it is God's will that Paul decide himself, but only after carefully considering what is the most responsible course of action.

Stage 5 reasoning is the most difficult to describe, in part because we found so few examples in our research but also because such reasoning can appear to run counter to what are often taken to be norms for maturity and health. At Stage 5, God or the Ultimate Being informs and inhabits each moment and commitment, however profane and insignificant. The Ultimate Being is realized through human action, wherever there is care and love. Freedom and dependence, transcendence and immanence, all of the polar dimensions become equilibrated to produce a way of being that can at times seem strange and marvelous. The self appears both more and less than what it was at lower stages. Individuals at this stage seem unconcerned with personal security, and yet they seem the most secure of all. Freedom now is found in utter commitment and obedience, which to others appears as a loss of freedom. Wealth becomes poverty, and poverty wealth. Even sickness and suffering can be valued because of the opportunities they offer for feeling closer to what is Ultimate. An example of a Stage 5 response to the Paul dilemma is the following: "Paul should not go if that would mean his life would simply be his fulfilling the promise he made on the airplane. Whether he goes or stays is not so important; what is important is that he fulfill the larger promise to live, whatever that may mean in the many, many challenges he will find."

Taking these stages together, we see a growing need for autonomy and a deepening appreciation for the unity or "partnership" of opposites. From "the Ultimate Being does it," to "the Ultimate Being does it, if . . .," to "the Ultimate Being and humankind do . . .," and, finally, to "humankind does through an Ultimate Being's doing, which functions through humankind's doing" is a long road and a struggle because each new stage brings losses as well as gains.

The growth from one stage to the other is only possible if a number of conditions are met. Within this developmental sequence, the function—namely, belief—remains the same, but the structure must go through a process of disequilibration and subsequent restructuring. Here are the main conditions of growth: First, the individual feels that the old structure does not adequately help to explain situations that call for meaning making. There comes the time when most people understand that "making deals" with God does not work in the long run; what's more, the notion of "dealing" in itself begins to be questioned. For example, people typically are responsible for organizing a sufficient water supply and cannot resort to praying for rain instead of building irrigation systems. Second, there must be a subjective need for autonomy toward and within the connection to the supernatural. Third, it must be possible for the individual to reconstruct the given structural level and apply new elements of reasoning to many situations in order to differentiate and integrate the new mode of thinking. The point of departure for each structural transformation is a rejection of the old reasoning structure: "For a long time I believed that God punishes us for bad doings; nowadays I don't believe in that anymore. God is not punishing us; rather, we punish ourselves for bad doings." This typical statement describes the transformation that begins with the rejection of an inadequate or "dangerous" thought system that once was important to the individual. In this sense, rejecting an old structure means building an atheistic view of it. And, as illustrated in the following section, without the development of a new structure, the individual would remain within this kind of atheistic view that is defined by the rejection of former conceptions of God and the relationship between human being and Ultimate Being.

Empirical Studies

The following discussion focuses on validation studies of the developmental model of religious judgment, studies of conditions underlying development of religious judgment, cross-cultural studies, and studies comparing religious judgment and other domains of development (for example, moral judgment).

Validation Studies. The first study aimed at validating our developmental model of religious judgment was conducted in Grenchen, a middle-sized industrial town in Switzerland: 112 subjects, half females, ages seven to seventy-five, were interviewed using the three standard dilemmas described earlier. Figure 1 shows that the hypothesized age trend was supported for ages seven through twenty-five.

Figure 1. Age Trends in the Development of Religious Judgment

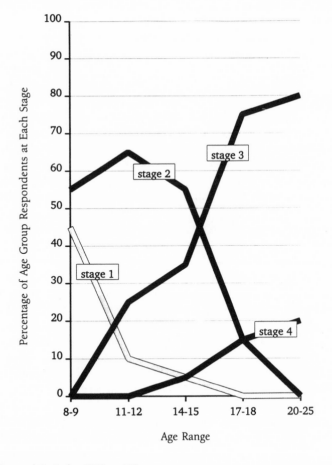

Source: Oser and Gmünder, 1968, p. 175.

In contrast, the trend did not continue past early adulthood. Rather, in late adulthood there appeared to be a regression to lower stages. The results pertaining to our older subjects were difficult to interpret. First, the sample of subjects between ages sixty-five and seventy-five was very small, so it was difficult to detect trends in the small data base, and the results may be subject to sampling error. Second, since this was a cross-sectional study, the data may reflect cohort effects. And third, the scores for older subjects may well be a function of the way older people are sometimes treated (mistreated) rather than a function of their age. (This issue is discussed more thoroughly in Oser, 1990.)

The results of the Grenchen study do not show significant differences between Roman Catholic and Protestant subjects. However, there are significant effects for socioeconomic status: Persons with higher socioeconomic status were more likely to perform at higher levels of religious judgment. Gender effects are mixed: Boys scored highest in stage development during the primary school years, girls during adolescence. In adulthood, this gender difference disappeared. Finally, a clear and positive correlation was found between stage of religious judgment and "interest in religious affairs."

In 1988, we began a longitudinal study to further validate the model. The preliminary findings of this study lend additional support to the hypothesized order of stages. As a variant on the longitudinal approach, we also have been conducting biographical studies. Brachel and Oser (1984) interviewed fifty adults about their own religious development. Most were well aware of the transformations that had taken place in their lives, and many offered specific descriptions of their previous thinking that correspond to our lower stages. Contrary to our expectations, these subjects attributed changes in their religious thinking to normal changes in the course of life rather than to critical life events such as personal crises.

In a second group of biographical studies, Bucher (1985), Brumlik (1985), and Hager (1986) analyzed the religious development of Rainer Maria Rilke, Martin Buber, and Johann Henrich Pestalozzi, respectively—all persons famous for both their work and their spirituality. Overall, the stage model of the development of religious judgment aptly described the religious (spiritual) development of these three people, indicating the usefulness of the model for analyzing written material as well as material gleaned from interviews and observations. This method may prove especially valuable in articulating the terminal point of religious development.

Studies of Conditions Underlying Development. To identify conditions underlying the development of religious judgment, we conducted an intervention study with two groups of adolescents, fourteen years of age, from the Swiss village of Malters. In the first treatment group, religious judgment was stimulated through discussions of religiously significant issues: Teachers confronted students with higher levels of responses to the issues than the levels reached by fourteen-year-olds. In the second treatment group, the same method was combined with variations in the content of the issues presented and with discussion about the nature of religious reflection. A control group of fourteen-year-olds received conventional religious instruction, where the emphasis was on providing information rather than on stimulating judgment. After three months of intervention, the treatment groups showed significant increases in level of religious judgment, whereas the control group did not. In another interventional study, Caldwell and Berkowitz (1986) showed that both moral and religious stimulation leads to significant maturational effects on religious judgment, whereas religious stimulation does not enhance ability for moral reasoning.

The context of religious development has been investigated by Niggli (1988). This author found that parents who supported, encouraged, and provided positive feedback for their children's religious judgments fostered religious development, whereas parents who did the opposite (for example, criticized and discouraged religious judgments) retarded that development.

A similar result was found by Klaghofer and Oser (1987). The findings of their study suggest that it is not the developmental status of parental religious judgment but rather the presence versus absence of a positive educational and open religious climate in the family that influences the growth of religious reasoning in children. Such results show us that the development of religious judgment depends on features of communication and social interaction experienced in religious and general education. For this reason, the context alone and the "religious capital" of the family alone (such as religious habits, religious discussions, and participation in religious events) are not sufficient conditions for stimulation of religious development. Only if both variables are integrated and embedded in a positive and communicative style of life and education can children and adolescents move toward higher and more autonomous stages of religious judgment. This finding has at least one important implication for religious institutions: Apparently, they lessen their chances of surviving as guiding and meaningful enterprises if they indoctrinate people by using only their inner "religious capital" and if they do not tolerate and even stimulate religious autonomy. The more these institutions encapsulate themselves in the claims of orthodoxy, the more individual religious development is hindered and even undermined. We do not yet have sufficient empirical data to back this hypothesis, but we expect to find relevant material in our longitudinal study.

Cross-Cultural Studies. Dick (1982) has carried out a number of studies supporting our assumption that the stage model of religious judgment applies cross-culturally. In samples of Hindus and Jains from Rajasthan, India, Mahayana Buddhists from near the Tibetan border, and a Christian group practicing ancestor worship from Rwanda, Africa, Dick found the same structures of religious judgment and, with one exception, the expected age trends. This was particularly interesting in the case of the

Figure 2. Stages of Religious Judgment for
Members of a Traditional Religion (Bantu Cult) and
Members of a Christian Missionary Group in Rwanda, by Age

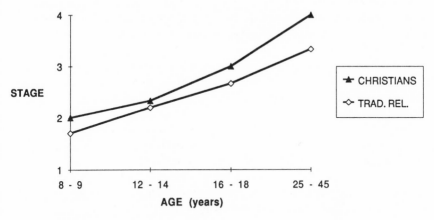

Source: Dick, 1982.

group from Rwanda because their theology does not allow for the possibility of God punishing someone who does not keep a promise. Yet, the younger subjects argued exactly this way. Figure 2 shows the Rwanda findings.

Religious Judgment and Other Domains of Development. There has been considerable interest in understanding the relationship between moral and religious judgment. However, research has not provided a clear picture of the relationship. For example, it is widely assumed that the development of religious judgment lags behind that of moral judgment (as measured by Kohlberg's stage model), and yet studies by Gut (1984) and others provide mixed results with respect to this assumption. A more sophisticated model is required (Oser and Reich, 1990b).

It is not surprising that the development of religious judgment has been shown to parallel changes and developments in children's worldviews. For example, Fetz, Reich, and Valentin (1989) found that lower stages of religious judgment were highly correlated with archaic views of the world, for example, heaven and earth relate to one another as top to bottom, and with views of the world's creation consistent with Piaget's concept of artificialism, for example, God made the world, even the buildings in it, much as a craftsman makes a piece of furniture.

Religious and Atheistic Development

We would understand the process of religious development better if we understood the gains and losses that accompany this development. The whole research program described above (and especially the intervention studies) is based on and justified by the idea that the development of religious judgment can and should be stimulated, particularly when it has been delayed. Increases in the ability for religious reasoning lead subjects to a higher religious autonomy, enabling them to be independently religious in a pluralistic world, even within increasingly centralistic religious institutions. However, we must not forget that such development is necessarily purchased through losses. The losses involve old sources of security: a parental image of God, religious dogmas, even faith in a divine plan. The gains are deeper knowledge, wisdom, and direction for living. From rather fixed ways of "being religious," we see individuals developing more open ways of thought so that "to be religious means to question passionately the meaning of life and to be open for answers even if they trouble us. Such a position makes religion something universally human, even if this is not the usual meaning of the word religion" (Tillich, 1958).

In terms of religious consciousness, the child who has abandoned Stage 1 and reached Stage 2 thinking has lost his or her naive notion of security warranted by an all-powerful Divine Being who guides him or her through the vicissitudes of life; what has been gained, on the other side, is the autonomy of feeling able to influence the Ultimate Being. The subject also has lost the immediacy of an animistic, artificialistic, and magical worldview, that is, the "first naiveté," but he or she has gained a more enlightened worldview. (The terms "first naiveté" and "second naiveté" invoke Ricoeur's concept of the development of symbolic interpretation. The "first naiveté" sees the symbol as if it were reality; the "second naiveté" dares to question the truth behind the symbol. See Ricoeur, 1980.) Even at higher stages, religious development necessarily includes losses. When a person's thinking is transformed from Stage 4 to Stage 5, the security of a salvation plan (Stage 4) gets lost, but the full immediacy of powerful religious experience is recovered. Theologically, the Ultimate Being is realized in such symbol-laden events as an embrace, a reconciling gesture, and a solution to conflict. Here, the subject has reached the so-called "second naiveté" that cannot be obtained without losses, ruptures, and often hurtful experiences. There also are losses at the medium stages of religious development. Especially in transcending Stage 2 thinking, people often lose their faith in God and become atheists or, at least, religiously indifferent. This leads to one of the issues raised in the introduction to this section: When talking about those persons, can we still call their reasoning "religious"? As an expansion of my earlier reply to critics (Oser, 1988a), I here want to state some considerations on atheistic thought within religious development.

The following thoughts are based on a recent interview study we conducted with subjects who explicitly declared their atheism. Preliminary results suggest that we have to distinguish four types of atheists: (1) Some people designate themselves as atheists when they do not believe anymore in what they believed before. This self-description seems to be transitional, so this type can be called "developmental atheists." (2) Some individuals call themselves atheists because they have quit as members of a church or other religious institution. In these cases, we could use the term "social or ecclesiastical atheists." (3) In other cases, individuals have thoroughly worked through their former beliefs, at whatever stage they are, and henceforth they deny any existence of a divine Ultimate Being. Instead, their worldviews may be variations of existential philosophy, Marxism, and the like. This type can be called "philosophical atheists." (4) Some individuals are characterized by an absolute absence of interest in religious affairs. Often they also lack concern for existential questions such as "What is the meaning of human life?" and "What is the destiny of humanity in the immense and incomprehensible universe?" Given that many societies foster superficial, hedonistic, and indifferent attitudes, and given that the major message of mass media is that knowledge can be split up in easy-to-use portions and that there is no such thing as universal truth, it can be expected that the societal context prevents many people from asking fundamental questions (Döbert, 1978) and, thus, that this type of atheism is widespread. Nonreligiosity of this kind can, however, go together well with mystical attitudes or quasi-religious forms of irrationality (from astrology to occultism). This fourth type can thus be called "easy atheists."

In the study on which this preliminary typology is based we interviewed subjects with respect not only to the standard religious dilemma situations but also to biographical events and transitions, focusing, for instance, on experiences with the Church and religious education. Instead of giving a detailed outline of results, I restrict discussion here to two findings.

First, as mentioned, developmental atheists are characterized by the rejection of belief systems to which they earlier adhered. Let us suppose that an individual has moved from Stage 2 to Stage 3. In order to make that step, he or she must deny the representation of God typical of Stage 2, including the notion that God rewards or punishes through concrete actions. Before the person has constructed a new representation of God, he or she necessarily develops an atheistic notion, essentially, an image of God that cannot support or establish a religious identity. Consequently, we can assume that certain phases of atheism are necessary, caused by religious development itself.

A special form of atheism occurs at the Stage 3 crossing. Here it seems that subjects who reject religious concepts and institutions are more likely to stay at Stage 3 than are others. For example, Schweitzer and Bucher (1989) show that in their sample of thirty-six adolescents and adults, among the twelve who reasoned at the Stage 3 level, nine rejected religiosity or Church-oriented thinking. In this sample, all subjects who totally rejected religiosity were scored at Stage 3.

Second, most of the individuals in our sample who understood themselves as atheists showed some idea of an Ultimate Reality when interviewed about religious dilemmas or contingency situations and when confronted with fundamental questions concerning the meaning of human existence. Frequently, the most important feature in the atheistic attitude of these subjects was that they solved the dilemmas and answered such questions without reference to a representation of God as it is understood by churches or other religious institutions. Most of the subjects in a study by Achermann (1981) were not rejecting faith per se but rather the Church as an institution, religious customs, the secular power of religions, and so on. Other atheists, with a more elaborated view, put something else in the place of such representations of God and referred, instead, to some other entities that henceforth performed the equivalent function. For example, a young woman denied the existence of the Christian God but articulated the idea that all things depend on nature, and that we have to worship nature for this reason. She did not know that also within the Christian tradition there exists a tradition of devotion to nature. Other, and most serious, atheists referred to social ideals that more or less can be pursued by political engagement. Achermann (1981) constructed a stage theory of the development of atheistic thinking that suggests a progression from (materialistic) determinism to belief in a global changeability of social affairs. From the point of view of religious socialization, most atheists (83 percent) felt that religious education never helped them to deal with relevant or critical life events (see Buggle, 1990).

Question of Universality

The issue of atheism is deeply connected to the question of universality of the stages of religious judgment. This question refers not only to the cross-cultural validity of the stage scheme but also to the viability of the notion of a religious "mother structure" that cannot be reduced to some other kind of thought structure, such as the structure of moral reasoning. By this definition, a religious mother structure is a kind of subjective *theologia naturalis* (natural theology), a capacity to deal with the seven polar dimensions in life situations in a subjectively necessary way. In this sense, we can assume that each individual is religious. This assumption, however, is a very global supposition calling for certain distinctions.

First, I believe that there is a religious mother structure that is represented in the way individuals relate the Ultimate Reality to their own thinking and acting. The ontological and anthropological conditions, on the one hand, are given by the way subjects experience contingency, weakness, surprise, change, and limits in life. The culture-specific content in different societies, on the other hand, influences the mother structure and is given by religious traditions and by the culture's symbols, rites, and typical interpretations. Depending on the forms of religious socialization, which may change from generation to generation, and on subjects' sensitivity to religiously relevant experiences and questions, contextual factors shape the mother structure, which itself defines the quality of the respective stage of religious development.

Second, a distinction must be made with respect to what we call negative religious judgment, for example, "I do not believe in God because if there was a God, he would help the poor, or there would be more justice in the world." The negative form of stating a judgment corresponds to the positive form, that is, it is based on the same organization of elements. The same elements, for example, the notion that God's actions are manifested in concrete, observable events can be utilized to apologetically assume or to deny God's existence. Even at the highest stage of development and for the most sophisticated people, there is a daily challenge to make sense of life and a daily temptation to focus on secular interpretations of events.

Third, a cultural distinction is needed to properly frame the universality of the developmental stage hierarchy. Although our cross-cultural data showed age-related development across samples, the rates of growth clearly depended on cultural and religious contextual factors. Development is faster in modern ("enlightened") societies than in traditional societies, especially in those traditional societies characterized by orthodoxy. In the latter, individuals conceive of religious rules as rigidly as they do moral rules, whereas in enlightened societies liberally educated individuals tend to see religious rules as matters of personal decision making.

Fourth, a distinction must be made with respect to the universality of stage-typical reasoning. From our perspective, only Stage 5 reasoning can be fully universal and at the same time serve to establish a firm religious identity. At this stage, the central features of revelation are understood as the common essence of all religions, however different their belief systems may be. For this reason Stage 5 thinkers can be perceived as the most promising hope for religious peace in the world.

Multidirectionality of Religiosity and Limits of Theory

Interviews with the subjects at different ages about the courses of their lives showed that variations in context or setting have an enormous influence on the development of religious judgment. Persons at Stage 3 who grew up in a traditional religious setting frequently rejected the standards of this setting, starting from denial of a personalized divine transcendence in attempting to build their own identities. On the other hand, people at the same stage who grew up in a cold, rational setting, frequently followed mystical tracks, for example, showed some kind of New Age religiosity or joined religious groups with a strong reference to a religious leader and to a personal transcendence. Thus, the courses of individual development strongly depend on biographical circumstances (Brachel and Oser, 1984). Clearly, we do not yet know enough about the multidirectionality of religious development. We shall have to elaborate our theory on the basis of further research, probably in such a way that religious symbols, religious acts, religious justifications, and religious relationships to the Ultimate Being are seen as embedding and differentiating the structural core of stages of religious development. Additionally, we shall have to improve our understanding of the developmental process. For instance, it can be expected that there are focal points of development: During certain time periods, subjects develop more in one domain of thinking (for example, social cognition) than in others (for example, moral or religious reasoning). These focal points have to be identified in order to understand cross-domain influences.

While we are well aware of the limits of our theory of religious development, some of them are an unavoidable consequence of inherent features of theory building within developmental psychology. A structural-developmental theory cannot give sufficient information about the necessary and optimal educational situations that stimulate religious development. Our theory does not say anything about theological models representing the fifth stage. Nor does it explain the sociological and motivational conditions for religious growth or stagnation. But it does address the logic of religious autonomy, the profound relationships people have with God, the conceptions individuals at different levels of judgment have about the relationship between science and religion, the religious understanding of texts, rites, and cults (Bucher, 1990), and the possibility of being free and religious at the same time in a modern, enlightened society. Our goal is to show that one can be religious, rational, and oriented to a lasting meaning (re-ligere) and still be free, committed, and self-guided. So while it is important to see the limitations of a theory, some of them will have to be accepted as necessary and maybe even insurmountable. In general, a theory that claims to explain all will not explain much. As such, a theory's explanatory power depends on its limitations in scope.

References

Achermann, M. "Kognitive Argumentationsfiguren des religiösen Urteils bei Atheisten" [Cognitive argumentation patterns of religious judgment among atheists]. Lizentiatsarbeit (unpublished thesis), Pädagogisches Institut der Universität Fribourg, Fribourg, Switzerland, 1981.
Brachel, H. U., von, and Oser, F. Kritische Lebensereignisse und religiöse Strukturtransformationen [Critical life events and transformation of religious structures]. Bericht zur Erziehungswissenschaft, nr. 43 [Report on educational research, no. 43]. Fribourg, Switzerland: Pädagogisches Institut der Universität Fribourg, 1984.
Broughton, J. M. "The Development of the Concepts of Self, Mind, Reality, and

Knowledge." In W. Damon (ed.), *Social Cognition. New Directions for Child Development*, no. 1. San Francisco: Jossey-Bass, 1978.

Broughton, J. M. "Genetic Metaphysics: The Developmental Psychology of Mind-Body Concepts." In R. W. Rieber (ed.), *Body and Mind*. Orlando, Fla.: Academic Press, 1980a.

Broughton, J. M. "Psychology and the History of the Self: From Substance to Function." In R. W. Rieber and K. Salzinger (eds.), *Psychology: Theoretical-Historical Perspectives*. Orlando, Fla.: Academic Press, 1980b.

Brumlik, M. "Die religiöse Entwicklung von Martin Buber" [The religious development of Martin Buber]. Unpublished manuscript, Pädagogisches Institut der Universität Fribourg, Fribourg, Switzerland, 1985.

Bucher, A. A. *Die religiöse Entwicklung des Dichters Rainer Maria Rilke* [The religious development of the poet Rainer Maria Rilke]. Bericht zur Erziehungswissenschaft, nr. 52 [Report on educational research, no. 52]. Fribourg, Switzerland: Pädagogisches Institut der Universität Fribourg, 1985.

Bucher, A. A. *Gleichnisse verstehen lernen: Strukturgenetische Untersuchungen zur Rezeption synoptischer Parabeln* [Learning to understand parables: Research, from a structural-genetic perspective, into the reception of synoptic parables]. Fribourg, Switzerland: Universitätsverlag, 1990.

Buggle, F. "Wie sehen dezidierte Atheisten ihre eigene religiöse Sozialisation, ihre Ablösung von der Kirche und Religion und ihre aktuelle Befindlichkeit? Ergebnisse einer empirischen Untersuchung" [How do decided atheists see their religious socialization, their separation from church and religion, and their present well-being? Results of an empirical study]. Colloquium paper presented at the Pädagogische Institut der Universität Fribourg, Fribourg, Switzerland, 1990.

Caldwell, J. A., and Berkowitz, M. W. "The Development of Religious and Moral Thinking in a Religious Education Program." Paper presented at the annual meeting of the American Educational Research Association, San Francisco, April 16–20, 1986. (German translation in *Unterrichtswissenschaft*, 1986, *15*, 157–176.)

Dick, A. "Drei transkulturelle Erhebungen des religiösen Urteils, eine Pilotstudie" [Three transcultural inquiries into religious judgment: A pilot study]. Lizentiatsarbeit (unpublished thesis), Pädagogisches Institut der Universität Fribourg, Fribourg, Switzerland, 1982.

Döbert, R. "Sinnstiftung ohne Sinnsystem?" [Meaning making without a meaning system?]. In W. Fischer and W. Marhold (eds.), *Religionssoziologie als Wissenssoziologie* [Sociology of religion as sociology of knowledge]. Stuttgart, Germany: Kohlhammer, 1978.

Durkheim, E. *Les formes élémentaires de la vie religieuse*. Paris: Presses Universitaires de France, 1915. *The Elementary Forms of the Religious Life*. London: Allen & Unwin, 1968.

Eliade, M. *Das Heilige und das Profane*. Reinbek bei Hamburg, Germany: Rowohet, 1957. *The Sacred and the Profane: The Nature of Religion*. San Diego, Calif.: Harcourt Brace Jovanovich, 1959.

Elkind, D. "The Child's Conception of His Religious Identity." *Lumen Vitae*, 1964a, *19*, 635–646.

Elkind, D. "Piaget's Semiclinical Interview and the Study of Spontaneous Religion." *Journal for the Scientific Study of Religion*, 1964b, *4*, 40–47.

Elkind, D. "The Origin of Religion in the Child." *Review of Religious Research*, 1970, *12*, 35–42.

Elkind, D. "The Development of Religious Understanding in Children and Adolescents." In M. P. Strommen (ed.), *Research on Religious Development: A Comprehensive Handbook*. New York: Hawthorn, 1971.

Fetz, R. L. "Naturdenken beim Kind und bei Aristoteles. Fragen einer genetischen Ontologie" [Natural thought of children and as seen by Aristotle: Questions of a genetic ontology]. *Tijdschrift voor Filosofie* [Journal of philosophy], 1982, *44* (3), 473-513.

Fetz, R. L. "Die Himmelssymbolik in Menschheitsgeschichte und individueller Entwicklung" [The symbolism of heaven in human history and individual development]. In A. Zweig (ed.), *Zur Entstehung von Symbolen* [On the genesis of symbols]. Symposium der Gesellschaft für Symbolforschung [Symposium of the Society for the Study of Symbols]. Vol. 2. Bern, Switzerland: Lang, 1985.

Fetz, R. L., Reich, K. H., and Valentin, P. "'Cosmogony' According to Children and Adolescents: An Empirical Study of Developmental Steps." In J. M. van der Lans and J. A. van Belzen (eds.), *Proceedings of the Fourth Symposium on the Psychology of Religion in Europe*. Nijmegen, The Netherlands: Department of Cultural Psychology and Psychology of Religion, University of Nijmegen, 1989.

Fowler, J. W. *To See the Kingdom*. Nashville, Tenn.: Abingdon, 1974.

Fowler, J. W. "Stages in Faith: The Structural-Developmental Approach." In T. C. Hennessy (ed.), *Values and Moral Development*. New York: Paulist Press, 1976.

Fowler, J. W. *Stages of Faith: The Psychology of Human Development and the Quest for Meaning*. New York: Harper & Row, 1981.

Goldman, R. *Religious Thinking from Childhood to Adolescence*. Boston: Routledge & Kegan Paul, 1964.

Gut, U. "Zur Validierung des Stufenkonzepts mittels des Kriteriums 'Moralisches Urteil'" [On the validation of the stage concept using the criterion 'moral judgment']. In F. K. Oser and P. Gmünder (eds.), *Der Mensch—Stufen seiner religiösen: Ein strukturgenetischer Ansatz*. [The human being—Stages of his or her religious development: A structural-genetic approach]. Zurich, Switzerland: Benziger, 1984.

Hager, F. "Die religiöse Entwicklung von Johann Heinrich Pestalozzi" [The religious development of Johann Heinrich Pestalozzi]. Unpublished manuscript, Pädagogisches Institut der Universität Fribourg, Fribourg, Switzerland, 1986.

Klaghofer, R., and Oser, F. K. "Dimensionen und Erfassung des religiösen Familienklimas" [The dimensions and perception of the religious family climate]. *Unterrichtswissenschaft*, 1987, *15* (2), 190-206.

Meadow, M. J., and Kahoe, R. D. *Psychology of Religion: Religion in Individual Lives*. New York: Harper & Row, 1984.

Niggli, A. *Familie und religiöse Erziehung in unserer Zeit. Eine empirische Studie über elterliche Erziehungspraktiken und religiöse Merkmale bei Erzogenen* [Family and religious education in our time: An empirical study on parental educational approaches and the religious characteristics of the learners]. Bern, Switzerland: Lang, 1988.

Oser, F. K. "Genese und Logik der Entwicklung des religiösen Bewuesstseins: Eine Entgegnung auf Kritiken." In K. E. Nipkow, F. Schweitzer, and J. W. Fowler (eds.), *Glaubensentwicklung und Erziehung*. Gütersloh, Germany: Gerd Mohn, 1988. "Toward a Logic of Religious Development: A Reply to My Critics." In J. W. Fowler, K. E. Nipkow, and F. Schweitzer (eds.), *Stages of Faith and Religious Development: An Intercontinental Debate*. New York: Crossroads, 1991.

Oser, F. K. *Religiöse Entwicklung im Erwachsenenalter* [Religious development in adulthood]. Bericht zur Erziehungswissenschaft, nr. 88 [Report on educational research, no. 88]. Fribourg, Switzerland: Pädagogisches Institut der Universität Fribourg, 1990.

Oser, F. K., and Gmünder, P. (eds.). *Der Mensch—Stufen seiner religiösen Entwicklung. Ein strukturgenetischer Ansatz* [The human being—Stages of his or her religious development: A structural-genetic approach]. (2nd ed.) Gütersloh, Germany:

Gerd Mohn, 1988. (English translation to be published by Religious Education Press, Birmingham, Ala.)

Oser, F. K., and Reich, K. H. *Entwicklung und Religiosität* [Development and religiousness]. Bericht zur Erziehungswissenschaft, nr. 85 [Report on educational research, no. 85]. Fribourg, Switzerland: Pädagogisches Institut der Universität Fribourg, 1990a.

Oser, F. K., and Reich, K. H. "Moral Judgment, Religious Judgment, Worldview, and Logical Thought: A Review of Their Relationship." *British Journal of Religious Education,* 1990b, *12,* 94-101, 172-183.

Power, C. "Harte oder weiche Stufen der Entwicklung des Glaubens und des religiosen Urteils? Eine Piagetsche Kritik." In K. E. Nipkow, F. Schweitzer, and J. W. Fowler (eds.), *Glaubensentwicklung und Erziehung.* Gütersloh, Germany: Gerd Mohn, 1988. "Development of Faith and of Religious Judgment: Hard or Soft Stages?" In J. W. Fowler, K. E. Nipkow, and F. Schweitzer (eds.), *Stages of Faith and Religious Development: An Intercontinental Debate.* New York: Crossroads, 1991.

Ricoeur, P. *Essays on Biblical Interpretation.* (L. S. Mudge, ed.) Philadelphia: Fortress Press, 1980.

Schweitzer, F., and Bucher, A. A. "Schwierigkeiten mit Religion. Zur subjektiven Wahrnehmung religiöser Entwicklung" [Difficulties with religion: On the subjective perception of religious development]. In A. A. Bucher and K. H. Reich (eds.), *Entwicklung von Religionsität. Grundlagen—Theorieprobleme—Praktische Anwendung* [Development of religiousness: Conceptual foundation—Problems of theory—Practical application]. Fribourg, Switzerland: Universitätsverlag Fribourg, 1989.

Tillich, P. "The Lost Dimension in Religion." *Saturday Evening Post,* 1958 (50).

Fritz K. Oser is professor of educational psychology and chair of the Pedagogical Institute, University of Fribourg, Fribourg, Switzerland.

*Faith as a universal, dynamic quality of human meaning making
can be defined in terms of each individual's center of values,
images of power, and master stories. Faith develops in stages
toward a point of maximal individuation of the self and
corresponding minimization of the personal ego as the standpoint
from which evaluations are made.*

Stages in Faith Consciousness

James W. Fowler

Close to the heart of what it means to be human lies the dynamic process of finding and making meaning in our lives. Ernest Becker (1968, p. 210) once called us *homo poeta*, the creature whose distinctive feature consists in inveterate meaning making. This chapter paints in broad strokes the results of a decade and a half of research and theory building that have focused on the processes by which we shape our worldviews and form the convictions and values that anchor them. The stage theory of faith development stands in the tradition of constructive developmental genetic epistemology articulated by J. Mark Baldwin (1897), John Dewey ([1916] 1944), Jean Piaget (1976), and Lawrence Kohlberg (1981). The theory also owes debts to the revisionist psychoanalytic ego psychology of Erik Erikson (1963). The influences of theological and comparative religion can be traced to Paul Tillich (1957), H. Richard Niebuhr (1960), and Wilfred Cantwell Smith (1963). The following three vignettes, which give us windows into three lives in motion, together serve to introduce the stages of faith development examined here. (All of the names given in these vignettes are fictitious, and the details of the person's life situations have been changed to prevent identification.)

Faith in Motion: Three Vignettes

Roger's Story. A young man named Roger is speaking. He tells us about his adolescent years and a family in turmoil. There was a divorce in

---

The author acknowledges gratefully the significant roles of more than 500 persons who have generously given access to their meaning making in interviews by the author, his research associates, and his students across a number of years. Parts of this chapter have been previously published in the author's *Weaving the New Creation: Stages of Faith and the Public Church* (San Francisco: Harper & Row, 1991).

a northern city, resulting in a move to a southern state. Division tore apart the extended family, bringing anger and alienation. There seemed to be times of recovery: His mother remarried and the new relation lasted for a time. But then that broke up as well, and there were more moves. His Catholic faith was under stress. He said God was not supposed to let things like this happen to good people. He felt that his young life was in crisis. His way of describing his feelings about God in this period is interesting. He said, "God became lofty, distant, unavailable. The ceiling blocked my prayers. Faith seemed like it was static. There was nothing personal in my relationship with God, and yet I seemed hungry for it." Then he said that at age seventeen something happened to change things for the better. "I was invited by a girlfriend to a new church. In this community they talked a lot about a personal relationship to God, and I felt that God became a friend. I felt that life mattered; I formed new relationships in that community, and I felt like I was beginning to walk with God."

Marie's Story. From her vantage point of being twenty years old, Marie starts by describing an experience in summer camp when she was thirteen. She says,

> On the last night of camp there was a campfire, as there always is in youth camp. The dark night sky was beautiful; the sparks rose from the big campfire against the velvet sky; there was music. Different people told about what God meant to them and had done in their lives. We felt close to each other after an intensive week together. There came over me a feeling of unexplainable, universal love. I felt like nothing human was alien to me. I thought at that time I could even love Hitler if he were there. Out of that experience of closeness to God, I developed a kind of peace and love that I carried with me for the next five years. I seemed to know just what to say to help my friends. They turned to me as a kind of confidant and adviser. It was like God was in me, a part of me. But then, in the second year of college, I began to see the injustices of our world. I began to be aware of people starving in Bangladesh. I began to be aware of the brutality in Ethiopia. I began to be aware of homeless people in the streets, in the richest nation in the world. And for a year I dated a boyfriend who was an atheist. I could see that he was a very ethical person, a good person, yet he did not believe in any God.

Then speaking about her own present faith, Marie says, "Now God is more remote for me. I no longer automatically know what God would have me say to people. I am committed to Christ and his way. His principles and teachings are the truth about how we should live. But now it's like God expects me to be responsible. I'm studying psychology, so that I can understand people, and their personalities, and their needs, so that I can help them and help to make this world a better place. I'm involved in politics and nuclear disarmament and feeding the homeless and the hungry. For me, following Christ's ways means doing these things."

Carl, Jean, and Their Sons. We are seated at a table in a northern state with a husband and wife, Carl and Jean. Carl is a seemingly bluff and hearty man, a Texan by birth. In his middle-to-late forties, his face is flushed, he seems tense and keyed-up. His apparent buoyancy seems just a bit overdone.

As we get acquainted he tells us that he grew up in an evangelical Protestant denomination. He mentions the name of his pastor during high school, and we get a sense that he had been significantly involved in church activities while growing up. When he went off to college, and then to the Marine Corps, he says he left the Church behind. After he and Jean married and two sons came along, they joined a traditional mainline church, where they have been members for about eight years. Carl was a highly successful entrepreneur and recently had sold the computer-oriented company he had developed for multiple tens of millions of dollars.

Carl is speaking, "The last year has brought dramatic changes in our faith life. The Bible has just become very important for us. It has become the central thing in our lives. We have become a Bible-centered family." His father, Carl tells us, had been a very strict parent, "He did everything strictly by the book. But it is different with me." Carl said, "I have two fine sons, godly sons," he said. "They set me straight. They tell me when I'm wrong. They make me toe the line." (That Carl chose this direction in his talk was initially puzzling to me.) "We are finding that our old church is just not Bible-centered enough. We come there for Sunday School and services and spend most of the day there on Sundays, and it's like we work all day. Of course, we hear a good sermon, but it just doesn't give me any uplift. It's more like another day at work." Then he says with enthusiasm, "But recently the Lord has put us in touch with some of the most dynamic Christians you could ever hope to meet. They are Bible-grounded, Christ-centered Christians. We are just growing in our faith in unbelievable ways. Actually it was Jean who began our move in this direction. Hon [turning to his wife], just break in here at any point and explain," he says, without any pause in his talk.

Carl continues, more excitedly, "When all this began I was in McDonalds one day and some lines from an old hymn I hadn't heard since my boyhood in church in Texas came back to me: 'Thou are the potter . . . I am the clay,' and I said to myself, 'That's the Lord telling me, "I'm not through with you; I'm going to make something of you yet." ' But it was Jean who got me into this new relationship with the Bible. Tell them, Honey."

Jean, an attractive woman in her late thirties, has seemed withdrawn from the conversation until now. Responding to Carl's urging, she indicates, without elaboration, that she has been involved in a women's Bible study group. She indicates that it has meant a lot to her and has awakened her to the Bible. She shows a little more animation when she declares that their old church and its pastor were all right; she even expresses appreciation for that pastor's good sermons. "But," she says, "there is nothing solid there that you can really stand on."

Someone requests, "Tell me about the Bible study group you have been attending." Jean takes center stage at this point. "It is a group of women. We gather each week to study the word of God. I believe the Bible *is* the word of God. We do not rely on commentaries or interpreters who put their intellects into the Word and say, 'Well it says that, but it doesn't really mean that,' and then dilute the absolute word of God."

Upon further questioning, Jean becomes quite animated. She tells about how her group's reading of the Book of Romans took eighteen months. "We read the whole book. Then we took it chapter by chapter, sentence by sentence, and line by line. We have tape-recorded lessons from a leader who guides each of these steps. She stresses the importance of believing that the Bible is the *inerrant* word of God. For example, Jonah and the whale." Jean asks us, "Do you believe that story is true? Do you believe it really happened just as the Bible says? I do. If I didn't, if I thought it was just a story someone made up, I would be giving up my faith that the Bible is God's word to us just as he intended it, and that we can *stand* on that word without *any* doubt." Jean then pointed to the account of the feeding of the five thousand as reported in the synoptic Gospels. "I see this as a genuine miracle by Jesus. You can't explain it away as Jesus getting people to distribute and share the lunches that they had prepared but were not willing to share. I believe that Jesus took those five loaves and two fishes and, by praying over them, produced all the food and more that it took to feed that multitude of people. Jesus really can and does bring miracles in our lives. I believe that; I stand on that as my absolute foundation."

At this point Carl breaks in, turning the conversation back to their sons: "Their mother is really helping them grow up as godly men—godly boys. They straighten me out. Let me tell you: My ten-year-old was having trouble with a bully in his class who was picking on him. I just told him [expressed with surprising anger], 'If he does that again [muttered oath] you just knock his block off and fix his clock!' But then the eight-year-old said, 'But Daddy, Jesus wouldn't want him to do that!' "

Jean, eyes shining, then says, "My father was an army officer. We moved a lot. I just went to church when my friends did. As a young adult I went to the Catholic Church. But I just never got a foundation. Now for the first time in my life I really feel that my life is based on the word of God. It is the absolute guide for our lives, and I just want to share this truth with everyone!"

Faith as Construction and Commitment

How shall we make sense of these three vignettes? How shall we under-stand Roger's move at seventeen toward a relationship with God very much like the one that Marie gave up at twenty? What shall we make of the interaction between Carl and Jean and their sons? What will become of them as they look for and align themselves with a community of faith more compatible with Jean's commitment to the Bible as the inerrant word of God? Can Carl adapt to Jean's insistence on the Bible as the absolute guide for their lives? Can he continue to accept the "straightening out" that his "godly sons" administer to him? Will Carl find a vocation, now that he has sold his company, that will satisfy his deep need to have God "make something out of him yet"? As we work our way here through a description of stages of faith, we will refer back to our encounters with Roger, Marie, Carl, and Jean.

Let us begin by considering faith as a dynamic and generic human experience. Faith understood generically as a human universal includes, but is not limited to or identical with, religion. One can have faith that is not religious faith. Common examples include communism and what some fundamentalists call "secular humanism." A religion, as a cumulative tradition, is made up of the expressions of the faith of people in the past. It can include scriptures and theology, ethical teachings and prayers, architecture, music, and art, and patterns of teaching and preaching. Religion, in this sense, gives forms and patterns for the shaping of the faith of present and future persons. Religions are the cumulative traditions that we inherit in all of their varieties of forms. Religious faith, on the other hand, is the personal appropriation of a relationship to God through and by means of a religious tradition (these formulations are based on Smith, 1963; also see Fowler, 1981, pp. x–36).

Just as we can distinguish faith from religion, it is also important to clarify the relation between faith and belief. Belief is one of the important ways of expressing and communicating faith. But belief and faith are not the same, particularly in the historical period in which we live. Since the Enlightenment of the eighteenth century, many people have come to understand belief as intellectual assent to propositions of dubious verifiability. Or as the television character Archie Bunker once put it, spicing up a quote from Mark Twain (Paine, 1935, p. 237), "Faith is believing what any damn fool knows ain't so."

Faith is deeper than belief. Ideally, our beliefs are congruent with and expressive of our faith. But faith is deeper and involves unconscious motivations as well as those that we are conscious of in our beliefs and in our actions.

In speaking of faith as a generic feature of human lives—as a universal quality of human meaning making—I make the assumption that as human beings we have evolved with the capacity and the need for faith. Whether or not we are explicitly nurtured in faith within the traditions of a particular religion, we are engaged in forming relations of trust and loyalty to others. We shape commitments to causes and *centers of value*. We form allegiances and alliances with *images and realities of power.* And we form and shape our lives in relation to *master stories.* In these ways we join with others in the finding and making of meaning. Let us look at these three dimensions of living faith in more detail.

First, faith is a dynamic pattern of personal trust in and loyalty to a center or centers of value. What do I mean by this term "center of value"? We rest our hearts, we focus our lives in persons, causes, ideals, or institutions that have great worth to us. We attach our affections to those persons, causes, ideals, or institutions that promise to give worth and meaning to our lives. A center of value in our lives is something that calls forth our love and devotion and therefore exerts ordering power on the rest of our lives and our attachments. One's family can be one such profound center of value. Success and one's career can be important centers of value. One's nation or ideological creed can be of life-centering importance. Money, power, influence, and sexuality can all be centers of value in our lives. For some persons and groups religious institutions constitute dominant centers of value. All of these and much more can attract our devotion and focus our energies as centers of value. From the standpoint of virtually all major religious traditions, God or transcendent reality is meant to be the supreme center of value in our lives.

Second, faith is trust in and loyalty to images and realities of power. We are finite creatures who live in a dangerous world. We and those persons and causes we love are vulnerable to arbitrary power and destruction in this world. How in such a world do we align ourselves so as to feel sustained in life and in death? "The Lord is my Shepherd, I shall not want." That is a statement about alignment with power and the placement of our reliance on security. One could also say, "my stock portfolio is my shepherd, I shall not want." Or we could say, speaking as a nation, "The Star Wars missile defense system is our shepherd, we shall not want." Ernest Becker (1973) said that in the face of death, we all try to build *causa sui* projects, projects of self-vindication, projects that help us have the sense that we will continue on even after we die. When I held my first published book in my hand, I looked at it and said to my wife, "Dear, it's slender immortality, but it is immortality. It will live after I am gone." With what centers or images of power do we align ourselves in order to feel secure in life? The question of how we align ourselves with power to sustain us in life and death is an important question of faith.

Third, faith is trust in and loyalty to a shared master story or core story. In the 1960s Eric Berne offered his neo-Freudian theory of personality growth and change called transactional analysis. One of the key ideas in transactional analysis is the notion that each of us in early childhood forms a script, a kind of unconscious story that takes form in each of us before we are five years of age. This script, like a fate in a sense, shapes and guides unconsciously the choices and decisions that we make as we move along in our lives. A mastery story is a little like that. It often begins unconsciously, and gradually we make it more conscious and explicit as something to which we are committed. An acquaintance of mine studied prisoners in a federal prison some years ago and found that among those who had tattoos, 60 percent of them had tattooed into their skin some variant of the phrase "born to lose" as a kind of master story engraved onto their bodies.

Unlike the unconscious scripts of Berne and the fated label on the felons, however, a faith master story gives direction, courage, and hope to our lives. It provides life-guiding images of the goodness—and the God-ness—for which we are made. A master story shapes our consciousness regarding the character of the ultimate power and reality with which we contend, and how we should shape our lives with our neighbors in light of that relation. A faith master story gives us horizons of meaning and guiding images of what it means to be a good man or woman and a part of a worthy community.

Faith is covenantal in structure. We are not alone or solitary in our faith. Faith involves trust in and loyalty to other persons. But that trust and loyalty with others is confirmed and deepened by our shared trust and loyalties to centers of value, images of power, and stories that transcend us as individuals and bind us together with others. This is what we mean by covenant. Covenant is trust and loyalty, a commitment between persons and within groups that is ratified and deepened by our shared trust in and loyalty to something, someone, reality, God, or some set of values that transcends us. Faith always has this triadic, convenantal structure.

Faith, then, is the dynamic process of construal and commitment by which we focus our trust and loyalty, our dependence and confidence, in a center or centers of value, and on images and realities of power. In faith we find coherence for our lives through allegiance to an emerging, conscious master story or stories. Faith is an existential orientation formed in our relations with others that links us, in shared trusts and loyalties, to each other, to shared values, and to a transcendent framework of meaning and power.

Stages of Faith Consciousness

For nearly eighteen years my associates in Boston and Atlanta and I have been asking people to talk with us in depth about their centers of value, their images of power, and the guiding stories of their lives. We have been asking people to tell us something of their lives and pilgrimages, their journeys, to give us access to how they have formed and are forming their particular ways of making meaning. Out of that work we have analyzed transcriptions of over five hundred interviews. These interviews average about two hours each. In the course of an interview the respondent and interviewer, often strangers to each other, experience as unusual kind of

...cy and depth of dialogue. The interviews that constitute our cross-sectional data include an approximately equal number of males and females. There are representatives of every age cohort from four to eighty-four. Protestants, Catholics, and Jews, in numbers proportional to the American population, are represented. African-Americans are underrepresented, constituting about 3 percent of the respondents. Here, for purposes of continuity and comparison, I have chosen to illustrate the stages with examples from persons raised in the Christian tradition. Jewish or secularist examples could have been offered instead.

When transcribed, the interviews average twenty to thirty single-spaced, typed pages of text. From our analyses of these texts we have identified and continue to refine seven stagelike positions in the process of growth and transformation in faith. Here we look at the evolving patterns of constructive knowing that have come to be called *stages of faith*.

Primal Faith. We all start as infants, and much that is important for our lives of faith occurs in utero and in the very first months of life. We describe the form of faith that begins in infancy as Primal faith. This first stage is a prelanguage disposition (a total emotional orientation of trust offsetting mistrust), which takes form in the mutuality of one's relationship with parents and others. This rudimentary faith enables us to overcome or offset the anxiety resulting from separations that occur during infant development. Piaget has helped us understand infant development as a succession of cognitive and emotional separations in the process of differentiation from those who provide initial care. Earliest faith is what enables us to undergo these separations without undue experiences of anxiety or fear of the loss of self. Primal faith forms before there is language. It forms in the basic rituals of care and interchange and mutuality. And, while it does not determine the course of our later faith, it lays the foundation on which later faith is built. One can readily see how important the family is in the nurturing and incubation of this first stage of Primal faith. (For a detailed and nuanced account of the birth of faith and selfhood in this stage and the next, see Fowler, 1989, pp. 1–36.)

Intuitive-Projective Faith. This style of faith emerges in early childhood with the acquisition of language. Here, imagination, stimulated by stories, gestures, and symbols but not yet controlled by logical thinking, combines with perception and feelings to create long-lasting faith images. These images represent both the protective and threatening powers surrounding one's life. This stage corresponds with the awakening of moral emotions and standards in the second year of life. It corresponds as well with the awareness of taboos and the sacred, and with the struggle for a balance of autonomy and will with shame and constriction in the child's forming self. Representations of God take conscious form in this period and draw, for good or ill, on children's experiences of their parents or other adults to whom they were emotionally attached in the first years of life (see Rizzuto, 1979).

Such representations express the emotional orientation of children toward their world and the leeway, dependability, and support—or their opposites—that it offers them. If we are able to remember this period of our lives, we have some sense of how important, both positively and negatively, it is in the formation of our lifelong orientations in faith. When experiences of change or conversion occur at later stages in our lives, the images formed in this stage have to be reworked in important ways.

Some of the dynamics of this stage can be highlighted in a crisis case involving Julie, a four-year-old whose mother had been recently killed in an automobile accident. The following is part of a longer conversation between the minister of her church, where her mother had sung in the choir, and Julie. The minister visited Julie and her father regularly after the accident. He and Julie would often sit on the floor in the family room and build things with small wooden blocks while they talked.

JULIE: Why did God take away my mommy to heaven?

MINISTER: That's a hard one to answer, Julie. When your mother was hurt so badly in her car accident she was in a lot of pain. Maybe God did not want her to hurt so much, so he took her to be with him in heaven.

JULIE: But why did God make that man run into my mommy's car?

MINISTER: I guess I don't think that God made that happen, Julie. Sometimes things happen that God doesn't do. I think he probably felt very sad when your mommy was hurt.

JULIE: When Tabby [the family cat] died, mommy said that God took her to heaven. Didn't he take mommy away too? I want her back. Why doesn't God bring her back?

For Julie, her mother both mediated cultural and religious understandings of God and *was* her God, in terms of emotional attachment. As yet, Julie's God representation is a fragile construction, resting on the support of a significant other who embodies, if only partially, the characterization of God that she is beginning to formulate. Will Julie's emotional and cognitive relationship with God die along with her mother? Or will God become a kind of maternal figure who represents the possibility of a continued relationship with her dead mother? That she is willing to use religious language, even at age four, is a strong indication that she will struggle to make sense of her mother's death in terms of how she understands God (this vignette is drawn from Osmer and Fowler, 1985, pp. 201–205).

Mythic-Literal Faith. The emergence of Mythic-Literal faith is during our elementary school years and beyond. Here, concrete-operational thinking, the developing ability to think logically, emerges to help us order the world with categories of causality, space, time, and number. This means we can sort out the real from the make-believe, the actual from the fantasy. It becomes a time when we can enter into the perspectives of others, and when we become capable of capturing life and meanings in narrative and stories.

Some of the dynamics, and limits, of the Mythic-Literal stage of faith become visible when we look at the struggles of twelve-year-old Charlie, a boy from a religious family (see Osmer and Fowler, 1985, pp. 198–201). Charlie had asked his parents some questions about God but then had backed off, refusing to discuss the matter further with them. Since Charlie was moving toward the confirmation class in his church, his youth minister scheduled an interview with him as part of the usual way of coming to know the confirmands and their religious backgrounds. The parents mentioned their concern about Charlie's questions and withdrawal to the youth minister, who listened with special care to what Charlie shared about God.

During the interview it became clear that Charlie was experiencing a crisis of sorts. His Mythic-Literal understanding of God's activity in the world was breaking down in the face of a newly emerging recognition of the seeming incompatibility of the findings of science and his own religious beliefs. Here is a part of the interview dialogue:

MINISTER: Suppose a person came from another planet and did not know anything about God. What would you tell that person?

CHARLIE: I'd tell them that he was the Creator and everything. He created the universe and all that. And I'd probably show them the Bible.

MINISTER: Do you think that everyone believes those sorts of things?

CHARLIE: No, not everybody believes that God created the world. Sometimes I wonder if I even believe it. We've been studying evolution in school, and I can't understand how what we're studying there and what my Sunday School teachers say to me about Adam and Eve can really be true.

MINISTER: Do you worry about that?

CHARLIE: Sometimes. I'm afraid if I don't believe then the spirit of the Lord won't be with me anymore.

At various points in the interview, Charlie gave indications of a predominantly Mythic-Literal faith stance. For example, after he spontaneously brought up the topic of heaven and was asked to describe it, he responded by saying, "I think it's way, way out in space . . . circling all the galaxies and all that." Likewise, hell was described as being "in the middle of the earth, and they say it's just fire." But now his Mythic-Literal faith was crumbling, with some deep emotional consequences. Earlier in the interview Charlie expressed his fear that the "spirit of the Lord" would no longer be with him. This proved to be a recurrent theme in the interview. When asked what sorts of things made him feel bad, Charlie replied, "When I've disappointed God. When I do things or say things or think things that I shouldn't." The interview continued:

MINISTER: What happens when we really disappoint him?
CHARLIE: He takes his spirit out of you.
MINISTER: Has that ever happened to you?
CHARLIE: Yeah.
MINISTER: When does it happen?
CHARLIE: Different times. There's this song that we're singing in choir. It's a beautiful song. It's weird. It makes me sort of, my eyes start watering and all . . . I feel really empty. It's called "Here Am I, Send Me," and it's just like asking God to send me into his hands or something.
MINISTER: I wonder why that makes you feel empty.
CHARLIE: It makes me feel like he's left me . . . like I'm not close to God as I used to be. I don't know if he's going to send me. I don't know what I think about him anymore.

Charlie is experiencing the beginning of a shift in the way he structures and relates to his centers of value and meaning. In his own way, Charlie is experiencing the void. We can see parallels between Charlie's experiences and those of Roger, who, in this same period of his life, experienced the breakup of his family and remembered that God "became lofty, distant, unavailable."

What may not be apparent, at first glance, is the way the structuring qualities of the Mythic-Literal stage also underlie Jean's deep attachment to the Bible as the inerrant word of God, and as the absolute foundation on which she can stand. In her total commitment to a literal dependence on the Bible she has found the foundation that her life never had before. This foundation fulfills both emotional and cognitive needs. The continuation of her marriage to Carl, in many ways, seems to depend on his willingness to join her in this commitment to a Bible-centered family life, and to the rearing of godly sons. What will happen when their boys begin to deal with the issues faced by Charlie and Roger? And how will Carl, so hungry for a sense of vocation and seemingly so devoted to her, adhere to the emotional and cognitive fixedness of her leadership in the family's life of faith?

Synthetic-Conventional Faith. This stage characteristically begins to take form in early adolescence. The emergence of formal operational thinking opens the way for reliance on abstract ideas and concepts for making sense of one's world. The person can now reflect on past experiences and examine them for meaning and pattern. At the same time, concerns about one's personal future, one's identity, one's work, career, or vocation, and one's personal relationships become important. These new cognitive abilities make possible mutual, interpersonal perspective taking. Here, in friendship or in the first intimacy of "puppy love," we begin to be aware of the mirroring of self provided by the responses of others whose feelings about us matter. "I see you seeing me: I see the me I think you see." As we begin to have the burden and the possibility of seeing ourselves as others see us, and as we confront the task of integrating these multiple experiences of self brought by our relationships with different persons, we face in conscious ways the struggle for identity. At the same time we begin to construct an awareness of our interiority and that of others. We are newly and deeply interested in "personality." New steps toward interpersonal intimacy and relationship result.

These newly personal relations with significant others correlate with a hunger for a personal relationship to God in which we feel ourselves to be known and loved in deep and comprehensive ways. Roger's story reflects this hunger when at seventeen he found a church community that invited him to share in this kind of personal relationship to God, and he began to experience the "friendship" of God. In this respect Marie's account of her early adolescent relationship with God seems even more profound. Apparently, her experience of God at the campfire, and in other contexts during her adolescence, led to a deep integration of God into her personality, so that for years after she "seemed to know just what to say to help [her] friends." It was, she said, "like God was in me, a part of me."

Parallel with the task of integrating a set of images of the self into a sense of identity, the person forming Synthetic-Conventional faith must form a set of beliefs, values, and commitments that provides orientation and courage for living. This shaping of a worldview and its values proceeds as adolescents encounter persons and contexts that offer stories, ideals, belief systems, rituals, disciplines, and role models that can capture and fund their imaginations and hunger for adult truth. A culture is in deep jeopardy when it no longer can provide encounters for young people with persons and communities who can satisfy the need for role models committed to lives of truth. Synthetic-conventional faith, in such a culture, risks becoming a tacit amalgamation of values, commended subliminally by the advertising industry and coupled with an unthinking allegiance to the empty dogma that all values are individual choices and are therefore relative. Every adolescent deserves a viable and vital Synthetic-Conventional ethos for the formation of faith.

Individuative-Reflective Faith. To reach this stage, two important movements of self have to occur. First, we have to question, examine, and reconstitute the values and beliefs that we have formed to that point in our lives. They become explicit commitments, rather than tacit commitments. "Tacit" means unconsidered, unexamined, uncritically approved. "Explicit" means consciously chosen and critically supported commitments.

This process of making our commitments explicit usually involves a "demythologization." In a way that parallels the Enlightenment of the eighteenth century, we engage in critical analysis and reflection upon the symbols, rituals, myths, and beliefs that mediate and express our traditions of faith. Through such analysis we interrogate their meanings and try to translate them into conceptual formulations. In doing so, we gain clarity about our faith; we gain precision in our understanding and its articulation. At the same time, however, we lose our availability to some of the power of symbol, myth, and ritual mediating our relations to the holy.

This critical and reflective examination of our faith heritages does not mean that one must give up being an Episcopal Christian, or an Orthodox Jew, or a Sunni Muslim. But it does mean that now one maintains that commitment and identity by choice and explicit assent rather than by fate or tacit commitment. In John Westerhoff's (1976) adaptation of faith development theory he names this dynamic of the Individuative-Reflective stage "owned faith."

Second, the Individuative-Reflective stage requires us to claim what I call an "executive ego." In the previous stage of Synthetic-Conventional faith, we can say that a person's identity is largely shaped by her or his roles and relationships. In that stage, "I am my roles and relationships." My "I" is defined by the composite of the roles I play and the relations in which I derive and maintain my identity. In moving to the Individuative-Reflective stage, I have to face and answer such questions as, Who am I when I am not defined by being my parents' son or daughter? Who am I when I am not defined by being so-and-so's spouse? Who am I when I am not defined by the work I do? Who is the "I" that has those roles and relations but is not fully expressed by any one of them?

The task of the Individuative-Reflective stage is to put in place an executive ego, the "I" who manages and "has" all these roles and relations, yet is not identical with any one of them. The task is thus to take charge of one's own life. It means claiming a new quality of autonomy and responsibility. This does not necessarily mean "individualism," though in this country it is often interpreted in individualistic ways. It does mean the exercise of responsibility and choice in regard to the communities to which we belong. In making choices, we also exclude other options. There is a dichotomizing, either/or quality to the commitments of this stage.

Marie's account of what she is experiencing at twenty gives us a window into the transition into the Individuative-Reflective stage. Testifying that God now seems more remote to her, she speaks from a perspective in which the world has lost much of its enchantment. She states her allegiance to Christ and his way in terms of the principles and teachings that lead her to political responsibility and preparation for vocational living in which she can help people and "make this world a better place." Her forming clarity about identity, beliefs, commitments, and vocation seems to have required that she experience a kind of exile from the intimate relationship with God that sustained her with such assurance during her teenage years.

My sense is that Carl, in his forties and just having sold the enterprise that absorbed most of his time, attention, and aspirations in the first half of his adulthood, is also poised to deal with the questions—and the call to vocation—that are intrinsic to the Individuative-Reflective stage. Vocation, as understood here, is broader than occupation, profession, or career. It is the meaning we attribute to our lives and the significance we find in the totality of our roles and activities. It therefore involves the meaning of our work, our relationships, our private and public roles, and our use of leisure time. Both identity and individuation need to be understood in relation to vocation and to what our lives are *for*. While Carl has been an executive, it seems likely that he has not yet deeply faced the question of who he is apart from the roles of breadwinner, entrepreneur, husband, churchman, father, ex-marine, as understood in conventional ways. Therefore, he feels deep pulls as Jean recruits him so powerfully to join her in the Bible-centered family life to which she aspires on the strength of the directive teaching she gets from the tapes and her woman's group. His anger and frustration, concealed from himself perhaps, suggest that deeper urgings for integrity and the lure to present himself to God in vocation may make it hard for him to "submit" for long to his wife's type of church.

Conjunctive Faith. At midlife or beyond, frequently we see the emergence of the stage called Conjunctive faith. This stage involves the embrace and integration of opposites or polarities in our lives. Now what does this abstract language mean? It means realizing in our late thirties, forties, or beyond that each of us is both young and old, and that youngness and oldness are held together in the same life. It means recognizing that we are both masculine and feminine, with all of the meanings those characterizations have in the particular culture of which we are a part. It means a reintegration of our masculine and feminine modalities. It means coming to terms with the fact that we are both constructive people and, inadvertently or intentionally, destructive people. The apostle Paul captured this in Rom. 7:18-20: "The good I would do I do not do; the evil I would not do I find myself doing. Who will save me from this body of death?"

There are religious dimensions to the reintegration of polarities in our lives in Conjunctive faith. Here symbol and story, metaphor and myth, both from our own traditions and from others, seem to be newly appreciated, in what Paul Ricoeur (1969, p. 352) has called a second or a willed naiveté. Having looked critically at traditions and translated their meanings into conceptual understandings, we experience a hunger for a deeper relationship to the reality that symbols mediate. In that deeper relation we learn again to let the symbols have the initiative with us. The series of television interviews between Bill Moyers and Joseph Campbell called "The Power of Myth," on the Public Broadcasting System, touched this kind of resonant spot in many American viewers in 1988 and 1989. The *Spiritual Exercises* of Saint Ignatius have been for many an important source of learning how to submit to the reality and mediated by Christian symbols and stories. Ignatius's method helps retreatants learn to let biblical narrative draw them into that reality and let it read their lives, reforming and shaping them, rather than the retreatants simply reading and interpreting the meanings of the text. This process develops a second naiveté as a means of entering into those symbols.

Universalizing Faith. Beyond paradox and polarities, persons in this stage are grounded in a oneness with the power of being or God. Their visions and commitments seem to free them for a passionate, yet detached, spending of the self in love. Such persons are devoted to overcoming division, oppression, and violence, and they live in effective anticipatory response to the felt reality of an inbreaking commonwealth of love and justice.

As I understand it, the Universalizing stage of faith represents the completion of a process of decentration from self that begins with the emergence of simple perspective taking in the Mythic-Literal stage. Gradually, across the stages, there has been a widening of that process of taking the perspectives of others until, finally, those persons who can be described by the Universalizing stage have completed the process of decentration. In a real sense we could say that they have identified with or they participate in the perspective of God. They begin to see and value *through* God rather than from the self. This does not mean that the self is not valued: The self is included in God's loving and valuing of all creation. But the self is no longer the center from which one's valuing is done. It is done from an identification with the transcendent or with God. This decentration from self—a genuine participation in the quality of a divine being and love—leads to a transvaluation of a person's valuing and to a universalization of her or his capacity for care, for love, and for justice. Gandhi (Easwaran, 1978, p. 121) once wrote, "There comes a time when an individual becomes irresistible and his action becomes all-pervasive in its effect. This comes when he reduces himself to zero." And then, quoting from the last verses of the second chapter of the Bhagavad Gita, Gandhi said, "One is forever free who has broken out of the ego-cage of *I* and *mine* to be united with the Lord of Love. This is the supreme state. Attain thou this and pass from death to immortality" (Easwaran, 1978, p. 122).

The persons whom we identify as representing this stage demonstrate that quality of universalizing and inclusive commitment to love and justice in a sustained way. They live as though a commonwealth of love and justice were already reality among us. They create zones of liberation for the rest of us, and we experience them as both liberating and as threatening. Many of these persons do not die natural deaths because they engage in the dangerous occupation of confronting us with our involvement in and attachments to dehumanizing structures of opposition to the commonwealth of love and justice.

Faith and Its Operational Structures

While influenced by the psychosocial ego psychology of Erikson, the principal psychological tradition in which faith development theory stands is, as earlier noted, the constructive developmental work of J. Mark Baldwin, John Dewey, Jean Piaget, Lawrence Kohlberg, and their intellectual descendants. Piaget took the term "genetic epistemology" from Baldwin. The constructive developmental approach, as described here, focuses on the operations of knowing, valuing, and committing that underlie the dynamic pattern of interpretation and orientation that is faith. This psychological tradition is heir to Kant's ([1781] 1969) designation of the a priori categories of mind that provide the means to order and make coherent sense of the data provided by our senses. It is also heir to Hegel's ([1807] 1949) work on the evolution of consciousness and the stages of reflective selfhood. In contrast to the strict focus on the mathematical and logical models of intelligence that Piaget employed, however, faith development theory has tried to take account of the constructive involvement in faith of intuition, emotion, and imagination.

In order to operationalize the activity of meaning making that is faith, we have distinguished seven structural aspects that together constitute the dynamic characteristics of a developmental stage theory of faith. Analysis of faith development interviews to produce stage assignments proceeds by examining each structure-indicating passage in terms of one or another of these aspects. An overall stage assignment is reached by averaging the aspect scores. Recent statistical analyses of interviews with sixty kibbutz founders conducted by John Snarey (1990) provide strong affirmation of the construct validity of the system of structural aspects presented here, including reasons for confidence that the stages describe unitary and integrated structural ensembles. (For a full description of these aspects and the methods and criteria for interview analysis, see Moseley, Jarvis, and Fowler, 1986; Fowler, 1981.)

Table 1 depicts the structural aspects of faith development by stage. In reading the columns of the table, one can see the integrated set of structures that constitute each of the stages. In reading the rows, one can see the qualitative structural transformations that accompany and constitute stage change. Elsewhere I have spelled out the foci of each of these aspects and have provided an elaboration for each of the stages by aspects (see Fowler, 1986, pp. 31–36; Fowler and Keen, 1985, pp. 39–95). I include the chart here without further explanation due to space limitations.

Conclusion

Faith development theory and research have emerged as a part of the late twentieth-century effort to address and account for unifying patterns in the pluralism in persons' appropriations of religious and ideological traditions. This work seeks to take account of the relativity of construing and constructing life-orienting meanings while avoiding the trap of falling into the shallowness of dogmatic relativism. By incorporating both constructive and

Table 1. Structural Aspects of Faith Development by Stage

Structural Aspects	Primal	Intuitive-Projective	Mythic-Literal	Synthetic-Conventional	Individuative-Reflective	Conjunctive	Universalizing
Form of logic	Sensory-motor	Pre-operational	Concrete operational	Formal operational early	Formal operational full	Formal dialectic	Unitive
Symbolic function	Cross-modal	Archetype imagination	Narrative imagination	Associational	Conceptual	Mystic-critical	Participative
Moral reason	Intuition of standards	Punishment-reward	Fairness, reciprocity	Interpersonal expectations	Societal rules, roles, laws	Procedural justice	Universal care and justice
Perspective taking	Affect attunement	Rudimentary empathy	Construct other's interests	Mutual interpersonal	Third-person, systemic	Intersystemic multiple	Transcendental
Locus of authority	Bonding	Attachment, power	Authority roles, relations	Group consensus, charisma tradition	Self-judgment, selective norms	Balance self-judge and reconstituted tradition	Transcends ego-striving, principle of being
Bounds of social awareness	Primal others	Family, nurturing environment	"Those like us"	Composite of face-to-face groups	Beyond tribe, ideological construal	Extended identification in time and culture	Genuine cosmic solidarity
Form of world coherence	Presymbolic, proto-rituals	Episodic	Narrative dramatic	Tacit system, symbolic	Explicit system, conceptual	Multisystemic, symbolic, and conceptual	Unitive actuality, cosmological integration

evolutionary perspectives, the theory and research are consonant with the epistemological breakthroughs inaugurated by the Enlightenment and by the nineteenth century. With its account of the Conjunctive stage, faith development theory moves beyond Cartesian subject-objective dichotomization toward a hermeneutical perspective, such as articulated in many disciplines and in contemporary philosophy of science (for an elaboration on these themes, see Fowler, 1988).

A growing bibliography of international studies and research using faith development theory and research methods suggests that this hermeneutical paradigm is growing in influence and is being widely tested (De-Nicola, 1991). Two volumes of critical essays focusing on this work are available in English (Dykstra and Parks, 1986; Fowler, Nipkow, and Schweitzer, 1991).

Religious educators and a growing number of counselors have come to rely on faith development theory for its provision of a set of lenses for understanding the patterns and dynamics of faith knowing and valuing. The theory has served in the shaping and testing of curricula and methods of education. It helps counselors, secular and pastoral, deals in nonreductive ways with the central human activity of forming and maintaining life-grounding meanings and of acknowledging relationships with all that has the value of the sacred in our lives. Thus, as research continues to refine and confirm the stage theory articulated here, there seems to be a strong, emerging practical affirmation of the validity and usefulness of this approach in the growing family of structural-developmental theory and research.

References

Baldwin, J. M. *Social and Ethical Interpretations in Mental Development.* New York: Macmillan, 1897.

Becker, E. *The Structure of Evil.* New York: Macmillan, 1968.

Becker, E. *The Denial of Death.* New York: Free Press, 1973.

DeNicola, K. *Faith Development Bibliography.* Atlanta, Ga.: Center for Research in Faith and Moral Development, Emory University, 1991.

Dewey, J. *Democracy and Education.* New York: Macmillan/Free Press, 1944. (Originally published 1916.)

Dykstra, C., and Parks, S. (eds.). *Faith Development and Fowler.* Birmingham, Ala.: Religious Education Press, 1986.

Easwaran, E. *Gandhi the Man.* (2nd ed.) Petaluma, Calif.: Nilgiri Press, 1978.

Erikson, E. *Childhood and Society.* (2nd ed.) New York: Norton, 1963.

Fowler, J. W. *Stages of Faith: The Psychology of Human Development and the Quest for Meaning.* San Francisco: Harper & Row, 1981.

Fowler, J. W. "Faith and the Structuring of Meaning." In C. Dykstra and S. Parks (eds.), *Faith Development and Fowler.* Birmingham, Ala.: Religious Education Press, 1986.

Fowler, J. W. "The Enlightenment and Faith Development Theory." *Journal of Empirical Theology,* 1988, *1* (1), 29–42.

Fowler, J. W. "Strength for the Journey: Early Childhood and the Development of

Selfhood and Faith." In D. Blazer (ed.), *Faith Development and Early Childhood.* Kansas City, Mo.: Sheed and Ward, 1989.

Fowler, J. W., and Keen, S. *Life Maps: Conversations on the Journey to Faith.* (J. Berryman, ed.) Waco, Tex.: Word Books, 1985.

Fowler, J. W., Nipkow, K. E., and Schweitzer, F. (eds.). *Stages of Faith and Religious Development: Implications for Church, Education, and Society.* New York: Crossroads, 1991.

Hegel, G.F.W. *The Phenomenology of Mind.* (J. B. Baillie, trans.) New York: Macmillan, 1949. (Originally published 1807.)

Kant, I. *Critique of Pure Reason.* (N. K. Smith, trans.) New York: St. Martin's Press, 1969. (Originally published 1781.)

Kohlberg, L. *Essays on Moral Development.* Vol. 1. *The Philosophy of Moral Development.* San Francisco: Harper & Row, 1981.

Moseley, R., Jarvis, D., and Fowler, J. W. *Manual for Faith Development Research.* Atlanta, Ga.: Center for Research in Faith and Moral Development, Emory University, 1986.

Niebuhr, H. R. *Radical Monotheism in Western Culture.* New York: Harper & Row, 1960.

Osmer, R., and Fowler, J. W. "Childhood and Pastoral Care: A Faith Development Perspective." In R. J. Wicks, R. D. Parson, and D. E. Capps (eds.), *Clinical Handbook of Pastoral Counseling.* New York: Paulist Press, 1985.

Paine, A. B. (ed.). *Mark Twain's Notebook.* New York: Harper & Row, 1935.

Piaget, J. *The Child and Reality.* New York: Penguin, 1976.

Ricoeur, P. *The Symbolism of Evil.* Boston: Beacon, 1969.

Rizzuto, A.-M. *The Birth of the Living God: A Psychoanalytic Study.* Chicago: University of Chicago Press, 1979.

Smith, W. C. *The Meaning and End of Religion.* New York: Macmillan, 1963.

Snarey, J. "Faith Development, Moral Development, and Nontheistic Judaism: A Construct Validity Study." In W. Kurtines and J. Gewirtz (eds.), *Handbook of Moral Behavior and Development.* Vol. 2. *Research.* Hillsdale, N.J.: Erlbaum, 1990.

Tillich, P. *Dynamics of Faith.* New York: Harper & Row, 1957.

Westerhoff, J. *Will Our Children Have Faith?* New York: Seabury, 1976.

James W. Fowler is Candler Professor of Theology and Human Development at Emory University.

Psychoanalysis occupies a unique position in the systematic study of religious development. Its method permits access to the subjective, individual aspects of the development of belief and of the relationship to the divinity, as well as to the critical moments of their developmental reorganization.

Religious Development: A Psychoanalytic Point of View

Ana-Maria Rizzuto

Psychoanalysis and the Functions of Religion

This chapter presents religious development from a psychoanalytic point of view. Psychoanalytic method and theory can only attend to limited aspects of the broad spectrum of religion that encompasses not only subjective psychodynamics but also complex social, cultural, and intergenerational phenomena. Psychoanalysis is optimally fitted to understand the private, individual aspects of religious experiences. Religious experiences are subjective, private instances of *attribution* of religious meaning to events, behaviors, and psychic acts. The same event, a destructive hurricane, may be attributed by one person to a natural climatic source, without any religious meaning, and by another person to an act of God, bringing a message or a punishment. The same behavior has a private religious meaning according to *the type of psychic act* carried out by the person involved. For example, attendance at a Sunday service may mean an act of communion with a loving God to a young adolescent in search of a protective adult, whereas to a rebellious ten-year-old it may represent an unavoidable submission to a dangerous God of power and might.

Psychoanalysis approaches development from a particular angle of vision. While it partakes of and has made many contributions to theories of human development, it attends specifically to the development of the human mind, the psyche. It conceives the psyche as the essential mediatory tool of a symbolic, self-aware, wishful being who attempts to integrate the progressive perceptions of a developing body, in the context of indispensable ministering adults enclosed in a particular cultural context of geography, language, myths, and beliefs. The essential task of the developing mind is to create from that complex matrix an exclusive and unique sense of personal self, of a subject of all the actions and experiences involved in the act of being alive.

All the structures and lines of development so carefully studied by developmental psychologies are the indispensable architecture supporting the edifice of the human psyche. The psyche, as a developmental formation, follows specific laws of structuralization, which have been described by many authors from many points of view. Granted such structuralization, there is, however, something about the psyche that goes beyond the structures that support it: the capacity after a certain age to interpret itself, the feeling and thinking subject, others, and the world at large. Such a capacity for interpretation and symbolic organization of perceived inner and external realities creates a new world, a *psychic reality* where the essential acts of living take place. The essential acts of living always appear in dialectic polarities full of tensions, requiring a constant effort of modulation and transformation of impulses, wishes, needs, ideals, myths, and beliefs. The essential polarities of the acts of living are to be dependent and to be autonomous, to love and to be loved, to be close to another and to have enough distance, to understand and to be understood, to make sense of oneself and to deal with many self-contradictions, to give meaning to life and to face its glaring absurdities, and to live knowing that death may come at any moment. The entirety of psychic life, from birth to death, is spent trying to make oneself comfortable in the crossroads of these many lines of tension. Personal religion is the broadest and ultimate context in which meaning is attributed to the essential acts of living in the most private realm of each person's psychic reality.

Religion (organized and personal) offers the opportunity for transforming representations of self and object into representations of God and religious characters. Integrated into a private or public belief system, such representations provide potential means for the modulation of the tensions inherent to the polarities of the essential acts of living by integrating the representations into believed transcendent realities, that is, a religion.

Personal Versus Organized Religion:
Religious Experience

Organized religions are cultural institutions that offer beliefs, rituals, and communal means of dealing with the tensions of life. They provide the individual with accepted ways of tolerating and integrating the polarities of life by offering symbolic and semiotic systems capable of mediating between personal life, transcendent realities, and the culture of the historical moment.

Personal religion is the private and idiosyncratic set of beliefs, convictions, and rituals of a particular individual that form the background for his or her attribution of religious meaning to events and experiences. The official God of organized religion may be very different from the God of experienced subjective reality, a fact often and easily overlooked. The source of the discrepancy rests on the chronology and complexity of developmental processes and their consequences for the formation of a God representation. The personal, living God derives from the time before religion, when the child forms in the first five years of life the basic self and object representations that are to color his or her entire life experience. This chapter focuses exclusively on this particular aspect of religious development, the God representation, illustrating the manner in which psychoanalysis can illuminate the subjective meaning of a religious experience.

Origins of Personal Religion

Organized religions preexist the arrival of each new child to the world. The child goes through the essentially formative first years of life without being developmentally able to grasp what religion has to offer. Since the most ancient times most cultures have considered the sixth year of life as the age when the child is first ready to be officially introduced to some formal religion. A conclusion of great significance for the understanding of religious development emerges from this observation: The basic psychic elements that children need to enter official religion, their individual sense of self and of others, their private manner of interpreting personal events—in short, the particular types of psyches they develop—stem from sources not directly related to religion. In fact, in dealing with the polarities of life from the earliest moment, the child has already formed complex representations of both parents, of the divinity, of the order of things, and, most important, of himself or herself as a unique individual. The private interpretations that the child has formed about these matters constitute something like a proto-religion, with a child-created private godhead, private psychic rituals to deal with it, and complex beliefs, all of which carry the force of convictions of emotionally lived experiences. These childhood convictions color the entire religious life of the individual and may reappear in adult life in normal and abnormal ways.

Normal religious integration of these childhood certainties works so smoothly that it is not easy to trace them. Their pathological emergence illuminates the otherwise hidden processes of the mind. A case in point is the intense preoccupation and fear experienced by a High Episcopalian college professor after receiving communion. She worried that by eating the body of Christ she was a "human meat eater," practicing cannibalism. Two events framed the context of her experience: Her elderly father was seriously ill and a group of Latin American students lost in the snow of the Andes had reported on television how, to survive, they had eaten the flesh of one of their dead friends. The students were practicing Catholics and had prayed much before their desperate meal. The college professor connected her worries to early childhood games with her father, in which they play at eating and being eaten, an ordinary game with small children. In her mind Christ, communion, love, and her father were connected by complex representational networks. Facing her father's death, she had hoped to be able to keep him alive in some way, some communion of sorts (Christ died, resurrected, and is present in the host for communion). She felt anger at his abandoning her and had a wish to "force" him to stay with her. Communion became the middle term to organized loving and aggressive fantasies (not without childish sexual overtones) of eating her father to keep him with her. Her mind condensed actual communion with her present-day and childhood wishes.

Psychoanalysis, with its method of free association and reconstruction of early and later psychic acts and experiences, offers a unique access to the subjective, representational, and affective components of all religious experiences. It illuminates the manner in which a given person interprets at many levels the subjective and transcendent meaning present in a religious moment. The systematic observation of many events, such as the fears and wishes of the college professor just described, may provide an overview of the ways in which individuals give personal meaning to ordinary religious activities. Psychoanalysis adds a dimension to the normative processes of development. While there is no question that psychic life is based on emerging, organized structures, and that they must be present for some religious experiences to be possible, it is also true that the structures condition only generic types of meanings and cannot generate personal meanings.

Generic meaning is the very essence of religion. For example, the college professor would not have been able to be so concerned about communion if she did not have the developmental capacity for high-level symbolization (generic meaning), the moral level of development (generic meaning), and her particular superego (personal meaning) to make unacceptable her unconscious wish (personal meaning) to incorporate her father (representationally linked to God and Christ, a personal meaning) by some form of physical communion. The example also illustrates the psychoanalytic notions of regression and repression as defenses acting during a moment of conflictual tension between *conscious religious intentions* and *repressed personal wishes* connected to them. The adult women regressed to the emotional and representational mode of her second and third year of life, when eating had a lower level of symbolization than that of religious communion. Repression defended the emergence of the ideational components of the wish but could not control the anxiety evoked by the preconsciously perceived connection between communion and "eating" her father.

The example illustrates the normal potential for transient partial regressions to earlier developmental modes of functioning, representing, reasoning, and feeling. In ordinary circumstances these transient regressions occur without conscious awareness. They are an essential function of the mind permitting the integration of past and present and the assimilation of new perceptions and experiences with those preceding them. Continuity of the sense of self is thus maintained in a back-and-forth movement between memorial processes and present-day dealings with oneself and reality.

The example also illuminates the role of repression of developmentally early religious thinking and feeling, which, in spite of being excluded from conscious awareness, continue to exert their influence on conscious belief. Repressed religious thoughts, feelings, and convictions color conscious belief without betraying their presence, until a moment of conflict makes their hidden influence potentially recognizable. The woman professor had thought as a child that it was very odd for Christians to "eat the flesh of Christ." She questioned her teachers and was reassured that Christ was really present in "a special way" in the Eucharist. She repressed the association she had made between playing with her father and many childhood fantasies of "eating people," until it reappeared in her adult life. An understanding of the multilayered meaning of her symptom offered her a highly personal manner of making sense of a life-lasting devotion to and intense feeling for the communion rite.

The entire communion experience of the woman professor took place in the privacy of her mind. No observer would have been able to notice it from her behavior. She herself was not able to make sense of her worries no matter how hard she tried because she was incapable of undoing by herself the repression of her earlier connections between communion and cannibalistic wishes. It was with the help of the psychoanalytic technique that she could give full human and religious meaning to her private manner (overdetermined by many factors in her as it is in everybody) of participating in the ritual.

Origins of a Personal God

When the focus of the researcher's attention is the private and idiosyncratic form that religious beliefs and practices take in the psychic reality of the believer, the findings reveal that the God of official religion may be very different from the God of experienced subjective reality (Rizzuto, 1979). *For the believer it is that subjective God that counts, because it is that God who is the specific object of a religious experience.* When carefully studied from the standpoint of subjective reality, God shows the attributes of a living person. His or her face, hands, and bosom are very significant to the believer; his or her disposition, good will, wrath, patience, and other traits of "personality" give the believer trusting reassurance or fearful expectations. These attributes are experienced not as conceptual ideas but rather as the believer's felt conviction that those attributes define the way God really is. The conceptual God of official religion and of many religious studies is but an aspect of the experientially richer God of private life.

For the researcher the primary question is this: How does it come about that God, a being who is never the direct object of sensory perception, acquires in the course of development such vivid psychic reality, such concrete traits, such well-defined "personality"? In other words, how does it happen that the believer "feels" God's presence and carries out a relationship and a dialogue with a being who is physically not there? This question is at the very core of religious understanding, because religion, at least as conceived and practiced in the West, is an attempt to relate to a postulated God, a *living God* (see Rizzuto, 1979).

If God takes the form of a living being in the mind of the believer, there is a need to understand the generic way in which the mind of a child, over the course of development, forms and transforms representations of living beings. God has to be a *particular* case of such generic process in two senses: (1) one among many and (2) different from all others because God is never present to the senses as are people. The study of the process of formation and transformation of object (person) representations in the course of development gives access to the specific study of the formation and transformation of the God representation.

An object representation, as understood in this chapter, requires description and clarification. Human beings do not know of life in isolation. No human can survive without the prolonged care of a maternal person. To be is to be with others. To be with others is to collect a vast number of complex memories about ourselves, others, and our mutual interaction. The memories belong to all the perceptual levels available: visceral (the milk that "touches" internally), proprioceptive (pressure and muscle sensations), sensorimotor, eidetic, and conceptual. The conceptual modality is the last to emerge in development; the others are present either at birth or very early in life. The representations can be transformed when new developmental functions call for mental reorganization. Such changes are givens of development and condition the form and type of representation at the moment of its last updating without erasing the previous modes of representation. Regression to an earlier mode of representation and to its private meaning is always possible, as the high level of symbolization of the Eucharist by the college professor did not alter its connection to earlier personal meaning obtained at a lower level of symbolization.

Object representations come always together with self-representations because to perceive a person is to perceive oneself in relation to the other. The representations of object and self become, through processes of updating, multilayered memories originating at all levels of development. The processes involved are "representing, remembering, fantasizing, interpreting, and integrating experiences with others through defensive and adaptive maneuvers" (Rizzuto, 1979, p. 75). "As memorial processes they follow the same rules of codification, storage, and retrieval which regulate memories relevant to the sense of being oneself" (Rizzuto, 1979, p. 75). Any representation has the potential to evoke many complex and contradictory feelings, each connected with a different facet of the complex representation or with memories of a different developmental moment. These self and object representations provide "the material and framework for all mentation" (Moore and Fine, 1968, p. 64). All mental functions, regardless of their levels of abstraction, must be mediated by these representations as the indispensable background to carry out psychic acts. The most abstract mathematical operation implies that the person is aware of himself or herself as a mathematician, and not as a lover or as a religious person. The awareness itself brings about the possibility of carrying out mathematical reasoning.

So far I have written about representations of real people in commerce with each other. But how do we explain religious commerce with a non-physical divinity that cannot be remembered because it has never been experienced? This apparent impossibility of explanation is flatly denied by people who have many memories of their relationships with a divine being. People say all the time, "I knew what God wanted of me, but I did not want to listen"; "God made me feel that I had to accept it"; "When I was at my worst God showed me that he was with me." Those who speak in such a manner remember with intense feelings their experiences with God. We need a theoretical construct to explain how such experiences are possible.

One theoretical approach that offers a solution to the apparent difficulty is in the writings of D. W. Winnicott (1953, 1965). Winnicott was not inclined toward theorizing but was adept at describing his manner of understanding the earliest of infantile experiences. In Winnicott's (1965, p. 181) understanding, "the [maternal] object is created, not found. . . . A good object is not good to the infant unless created by the infant. . . . Yet the object has to be found to be created. This has to be accepted as a paradox." What Winnicott is saying is that there is a need in the child to find a mother in the real world, while the child *feels* that his or her own creative powers have brought the mother about. To represent her is to create her from inside oneself. The description bespeaks the playful, creative power of the child. If true playfulness develops between mother and child, then a nonphysical space opens up in the child's mind and in life, a transitional space, where the mind can employ its many abilities for the creation of psychic realities. These psychic realities are as real as the physical reality in which we live. Winnicott (1953, p. 14) connected the transitional space with religion: "This intermediate area of experience, unchallenged in respect of its belonging to inner or external (shared) reality, constitutes the greater part of the infant's experience, and throughout life is retained in the intense experience that belongs to the arts and to religion and to imaginative living, and to creative scientific work."

Winnicott makes two essential points: (1) There is in psychic reality a transitional space for creativity where object, self, or any other representation can be a creation of the experiencing subject, which may or may not meet with an externally existing reality. (2) The transitional space is present throughout life, accommodates any new developmental function and any level of development, and is specifically apt for all cultural and private creations, religion among them.

The representational objects inhabiting the transitional space are all objects created by the imagination, transitional objects, even if they happen to coincide with reality, as has happened with some scientific discoveries. However, in themselves, the objects have illusory lives, given to them by their creators. They are not created anew from nothing. They are generated from the immense wealth of affect-laden, representational, memorial processes available to the mind of even a young child, who can flesh them out whenever there is a need for them. Young children (and so-called primitive religious people) are notorious for creating vast universes of transitional objects from monsters to fairies, passing through all kinds of humanlike animals. The representational object-making gift is not limited to children. All human beings have it until they die. Nowadays, we all, children and grown-ups, have become adept at populating the lonely spatial universe with E.T.'s and space people. We even manage to love or hate them.

The earliest personal God is a special transitional representational object created by the child from affect-laden memories of mother and father and the interacting child. The feelings evoked by the representation of God find their source in the child's belief about the type of event that takes place between himself or herself and God. If God is conceived as protective and loving, trust and joy prevail; if God takes the shape of any angry persecutor, he or she may be avoided in fear. The particular "traits" of God's character do not need to come directly from the actual parent. Rather, they can come from the child's interpretive action of what the parent feels or thinks about the child. The process of formation and transformation of the God representation continues throughout life, to the last minute of life, as shown by the well-known cases of refound belief in the trenches or in deathbed conversions. The rules that regulate the formation and transformation of the God representation are the same that apply to any object representation. In this sense, the God representation is a particular instance of a general case. Representations are transformed all the time, except when they are repressed. The transformations originate in multiple sources: psychic development of cognitive modes, levels of intellectual and emotional development, bodily transformation of functions and libidinal zones, personal transformation of modes of attachment and autonomy, new love objects, new stages in social and professional life, and events in the world at large. This multitude of factors may call forth in each instance a God representation that is not fitting for the moment of experience, for example, when a naive God representation, which has not been properly updated since childhood, is called upon to deal with the death of a parent. A major confrontation ensues that may require a psychic crisis to include in the God representation the lack of omnipotent protection that death implies, or that may end in the outright rejection of God and belief, a common occurrence.

Both the creation of a God representation and the finding of the God of official religion require a cultural context that offers the child a particular type of God. Children and adults do not create a new cultural God. They accept and adapt to their needs the God provided by the culture. For all practical purposes of official discourse and practices their God fits the cultural description. *It is only in the privacy of their psychic lives that the researcher finds the similarities and discrepancies between the God of official religion and the living God of religious experience.*

A question remains. From where does the feeling of convincing reality of a religious experience come? Two sources seem to contribute to it. First, a *private source* provides intense feelings of an experienced encounter with a divine being. This source is connected to the living and lived feelings linked to the representation of God and its origin in actual moments of affective human exchanges and their interpretations. This source defines the type of exchange occurring in the experience.

Second, a *public source* is the consensus of the community about the actual existence of the divinity, giving credence to its capacity to intervene in human affairs. This consensus is indispensable. No human being can believe in a transcendent God in complete isolation. Public belief is *a collective act of attribution of religious meaning* to the world and historical events, as the Bible illustrates so graphically. In the concrete moment of religious experience the contribution of each source complements the other in bringing about the intense sense of reality of God's perceived intervention.

When attention is focused on a people's living God, the question of the developmental psychologist is whether there is a normative process of development for the representation of God. The answer is yes and no. Descriptively, it is possible to present an ideal sequence of transformation of the God representation. However, such an ideal is not normative and cannot be used as such.

Descriptively, it is possible to postulate an ideal series of progressively transformed God representations following the general normative pattern of transformation of self and object representations. Psychoanalytic and developmental psychologists have observed the changes in self and object representations from the early total dependence on the mother to the autonomous, sexually differentiated, self-sufficient individual capable of assuming full responsibility for his or her own life and the lives of others (Erikson, 1959; Jacobson, 1961, 1964; Mahler, 1972, 1975; Blos, 1979).

Transformations of God representations affect and are affected by the actual interpersonal relationships of the people involved. Such relationships evolve from the early indispensable need for the mother to the mature capacity to love, understand, and accept another person as a different and independent being. The representation of God and the complementary self-representations of the person relating to God follow the same psychological rules that apply to all representations. In this sense, too, God as a representation is a particular case in point of a general developmental process.

The ideal developmental sequence for the believer in the Western world, where the Judeo-Christian monotheistic tradition prevails, can be outlined as follows: (1) a fully trustworthy being, (2) a good, tolerant companion, (3) a lovable and loving (even if a bit frightful) being, (4) a knowledgeable, good protector, (5) a being that can tolerate questioning and doubt while believers face the contradictions of life and the evil in the world, (6) a being who is there and who lets believers be themselves, and (7) a trustworthy being whose mysterious existence is not challenged (Rizzuto, 1979, pp. 205–208). This ideal series portrays the type of God representation that best suits each of the seven ages of life from birth to death (Erikson, 1959). The series describes the situation of optimal resolution of unavoidable conflict when belief in God is psychologically possible. This most favorable situation never occurs in actual life. Most people find insurmountable external and internal obstacles that interfere with the updating of the God representation to their respective development level. Besides, and most significantly, very rarely does a human being achieve such fullness of psychic maturity in ordinary human relations. Most people encounter many obstacles at each developmental stage and, therefore, do not find complete resolution of the issues involved in each stage, thus arriving at the next developmental moment hindered by unresolved difficulties. In short, none of us fulfills the developmental process as ideally portrayed. We are all a bit abnormal. The same situation applies to the God representation and the religious behaviors and experiences linked to them. Absence of belief is not in itself a sign of pathology, but rather an indicator of the vicissitudes of the process of belief. *Psychic maturity cannot be measured by the presence or absence of belief.* On the other hand, careful exploration of the subjective description of an individual's God representation and the vicissitudes of the relationship with God may reveal precious information about the type of psychic and interpersonal events that led to the particular characteristics attributed to God. In this sense the God representation has the potential of a projective test.

An understanding of an individual's God representation may provide, in turn, information about his or her psychic history and the types of obstacles that interfere with potential belief, or with the updating of the God representation. I am referring now to the processes of defense, repression, regression, and fixation of infantile wishes that may obstruct the transformation of the God representation and of religious behavior to a level more compatible with the individual's developmental moment. The knowledge of such processes could be of great help to pastors and religious educators in guiding people toward freedom from their religious limitations, or toward toleration of their limitations.

Conclusion

The concrete, *consciously* available characteristics of the representation of God in a person at a given moment depend on three factors: (1) developmental level of the representation available for the experience, (2) defensive psychic maneuvers employed at the moment to avoid distressing aspects of the representation, and (3) dynamic integration of the representation of God with the self-representation of the moment, in a particular situation in life.

A brief clinical example illustrates my theoretical description. A devout Jewish scientist believed in a God who was just and had, in general, looked favorably on him. He went to temple every sabbath and found peaceful satisfaction in the services. In the course of his analysis, many feelings about his parents, his analyst, himself, and his God began to surface. He was becoming very fond of his woman analyst and could not acknowledge to himself that he was experiencing a (transferential) wish that she love him, prefer him over others, and offer him sexual favors. All these wishes appeared in disguised displacement onto other "delicious" women, whose husbands or boyfriends were always "fooled" by him. One day he came to his hour in a great panic and began to cry uncontrollably, claiming that "God has cursed me." He was sure of the curse. His life was over. He would die soon, and even if he lived, there was no meaning to his life. His despair was intense, his conviction firm. When asked how it had come about that God cursed him, he said that he did not know, but he did know that the curse was for real. The curse did not imply any specific punishment or disaster except that God did not like him and did not care for him anymore. It took a long time to unveil how he came to be so convinced that God's curse was upon him.

To understand his religious experience during analysis, it is important to remember that analysis brings about a vivid regression to childhood moments and experiences that are felt to be real in the here and now of the analytic situation. The young man was reliving a particular oedipal moment in which he had had an intensely affectionate and (for his childish perception) sexual relationship with his mother. Some people had remarked then that he was "mother's little husband." He had been very proud of the situation and had felt entitled to special privileges. While he tried to remain a "good boy," he had developed many "sneaky ways" to get his mother away from his father and more involved with him. The father had become aware of his tricks and attempted to put him in his place, which in turn moved the boy to create more subtle ways of obtaining what he wanted. He felt the double satisfaction of getting his mother's attention and of outsmarting his father. All seemed most satisfactory, except his growing feelings of guilt and fear that his father would find out what he was doing and a terrible punishment would follow. Probably his father would disown him forever. The feared and terrifying confrontation never came, and his "sneaky behavior" with his mother was still going on in his adult life at the time he felt "God's curse."

Reconstruction of the events revealed that he had felt that the analyst (with whom he employed the same "sneaky tricks") was getting very close to figuring him out, bringing finally to the open the terrible confrontation he had expected since he was a young boy. It was during that moment of terror in the analysis, fearing the analyst, that God was called to psychic duty to pronounce the horrible curse. As a defensive maneuver of an unconscious nature it as a brilliant move. He could show the analyst the pain inflicted on him by God's curse. That would stop the analyst's expected punishment. The defensive move protected the relationship with the analyst by making God, and not her, the cruel and unjust chastiser. He had attempted to distract the analyst's attention from his guilty behavior by pleading for attention to his predicament as a victim.

The entire process was revealed as the same type of behavior he had employed to distract his father, and to require his protection from a supposedly victimizing mother. The God representation betrayed its direct connection with the representation of his father when he was between four and seven years old. It also uncovered the association between his learning about God's curses and punishments in Hebrew school and the chastisement he feared from his father. This childhood God representation, defensively made devoid of any protective or caring aspects, had been called to his conscious awareness in a critical moment of transferential urgency, when he feared he would be "caught sneaking" by his analyst. God's presence gave him dynamic room to maneuver in the analysis in order to avoid the expected punishment by the analyst. As a transient representation of the repressed past in the analytic present, God and his curse helped him to buy time to pacify the imagined, furious analyst. The example illuminates the regressive level (ages four to seven) of the representation, the repression (omission of the just aspects of God) at work within the representation itself, and the dynamic interpersonal function (to prevent the loss of his analyst's love) of the representation when it appeared in consciousness.

The young scientist's case illustrates only a transient moment of religious experience during psychoanalysis. God's curse was for him but an aspect of a broader and more solid texture of his life as a devout Jew. The magnifying glass effect of the analytic process brought to light aspects of his religious experience that otherwise would have remained unknown to him or to any observer.

Most everyday religious experiences are the result of a smooth blending of a personal living God and accepted religious beliefs and practices. However, when the imagery evoked by the God of official religion is not capable of linking up with the living God of personal experience, belief may become impossible or very superficial.

The value of psychoanalysis in understanding the individual's living God is multifaceted: (1) It contributes to the understanding of the development of religion by providing detailed information about the psychic processes that bring about the formation of the representation of a living God. (2) It offers a manner of conceptualizing the motivational sources of concrete religious experiences in the context of particular life circumstances and group beliefs. (3) It permits the establishment of an ideal sequence of modes of relating to a divine being, a sequence that parallels the progressive transformation of human relations in an ideal model of increasing psychic maturity. Such an ideal is not normative but descriptive. Personal maturity cannot be determined by the presence or absence of religious behaviors. (4) It is capable of clarifying the sequential transformation of religious experiences in the course of child and adult development by documenting the motivational sources and psychic functions of concrete religious experience. (5) It conceives of religious experiences as subjective acts of attribution of religious meaning to events and psychic acts. And (6) it describes religion as a societal and personal creation to modulate the intrapsychic and interpersonal tensions of the essential polarities of living.

References

Blos, P. The Adolescent Passage. New York: International Universities Press, 1979.

Erikson, E. H. Identity and the Life Cycle. New York: International Universities Press, 1959.

Jacobson, E. "Adolescent Moods and the Remodeling of Psychic Structure in Adolescence." Psychoanalytic Study of the Child, 1961, 16, 164–183.

Jacobson, E. The Self and the Object World. New York: International Universities Press, 1964.

Mahler, M. S. "On the First Three Subfaces of the Separation-Individuation Process." International Journal of Psychoanalysis, 1972, 53, 133.

Mahler, M. S., Pine, F., and Bergman, A. The Psychological Birth of the Human Infant. New York: International Universities Press, 1975.

Moore, B. E., and Fine, B. D. A Glossary of Psychoanalytic Terms and Concepts. New York: American Psychoanalytic Association, 1968.

Rizzuto, A.-M. The Birth of the Living God: A Psychoanalytic Study. Chicago: University of Chicago Press, 1979.

Winnicott, D. W. "Transitional Objects and Transitional Phenomena." International Journal of Psychoanalysis, 1953, 34, 2.

Winnicott, D. W. The Maturational Processes and the Facilitating Environment: Studies in the Theory of Emotional Development. New York: International Universities Press, 1965.

Winnicott, D. W. "Mirror-Role of Mother and Family in Child Development." In D. W. Winnicott, Playing and Reality. New York: Basic Books, 1971.

Ana-Maria Rizzuto is training and supervisory analyst at the Psychoanalytic Institute of New England, East, and clinical professor of psychiatry at Tufts University, School of Medicine, Boston, Massachusetts.

PART TWO

Specific Topics and Past Research

During adolescence, prayer begins to function less as a way to bend God's will to one's own and more as a way to search for better wishes, cope with difficult feelings, and foster a feeling of closeness to God.

The Development of Prayer in Adolescence

W. George Scarlett, Lucy Perriello

William James (1902, p. 464) provided the following simple, pleasing definition of prayer and its significance: "[Prayer is] every kind of inward communion or conversation with the power recognized as divine. . . . Prayer in this wide sense is the very soul and essence of religion." Given the central role that James assigns to prayer, it is difficult to explain why his account is so brief and tucked away in a late chapter titled "Other Characteristics" (of religion). Even more perplexing is that since James's time there has been so little written about the psychology of prayer. Prayer's significance to the religious life and the paucity of research on prayer require us to take a closer look at its forms, functions, and place in the lives of those who pray.

But how are we to understand prayer? To answer this question we need to look at personal (not institutional) prayers constructed to meet the demands of particular situations. And we need to look at how prayers develop. By looking at personal prayers and their development we can best hope to capture the inner dynamic of prayer, as revealed in its changing forms and contexts.

Our purpose here is to provide an analysis of prayer's functions and a particular model of prayer's development in terms of those functions. To clarify this purpose, we need first to say something about the issue of development and prayer because it is not at all self-evident that religion in general and prayer in particular develop into states we can call "mature."

The first author thanks colleagues at Assumption College who provided comments and suggestions, especially Neil Rankin, Diana Elvin, and Richard Lamoureux.

Prayer's Functions, the Issue of Maturity, and the Model of Developed Prayer

The legacy of Freud left us with a bias toward seeing prayer as rooted in illusion, an activity functioning solely to make us feel better by avoiding ourselves, our troublesome feelings, and our sometimes impossible predicaments. Freud would have us face reality stoically and rationally rather than remain propped up by illusions that soothe. From Freud's perspective, there may be a time in childhood when we need illusions, but maturity means growing beyond this need:

> I must contradict you when you go on to argue that men are completely unable to do without the consolation of the religious illusion, that without it they could not bear the troubles of life and the cruelties of reality. That is true, certainly, of the men into whom you have instilled the sweet—or bitter-sweet—poison from childhood onward. But what of the other men, who have been sensibly brought up? Perhaps those who do not suffer from the neurosis will need no intoxicant to deaden it. They will, it is true, find themselves in a difficult situation. They will have to admit to themselves the full extent of their helplessness and their insignificance in the machinery of the universe; they can no longer be the center of creation, no longer the object of tender care on the part of a beneficent Providence. They will be in the same position as a child who has left the parental house where he was so warm and comfortable. But surely infantilism is destined to be surmounted. Men cannot remain children forever; they must in the end go out into 'hostile life.' We may call this 'education to reality.' Need I confess to you that the sole purpose of my book is to point out the necessity for this forward step [Freud, (1927) 1964, p. 81]?

We have no quarrel with this perception that religion serves to soothe with comforting illusions. Our quarrel is with Freud's reduction of religion to this single function. From our perspective, development brings different functions that may, at times, upset rather than soothe. Nor do we disagree with the contention that adults should face reality head-on. But the reality faced in prayer may be a very different kind of reality than that faced on the analyst's couch.

Although Freud acknowledged the existence of noble and adaptive wishes, he saw them as conscious and a weak source of motivation unless individuals first faced the reality of ignoble and maladaptive wishes. We take the opposite view when speaking of prayer. We assume that people are as prone to denying what is noble and adaptive as they are to denying what is not, especially in times of stress and confusion when strong feelings prevent them from thinking about higher values and what is best for the long run.

Through mature prayer, then, individuals may struggle to make conscious what they *should* desire and what *should* motivate their actions. And when, through prayer, people focus (or refocus) on "higher" wishes, they at least have a chance of acting on them. The motivation to act may be weak but at least there is motivation.

To clarify this point about mature prayer, consider the following example: One of Abraham Lincoln's generals is reported to have said, "I pray God is on our side," to which Lincoln responded, "No, general, let us pray we are on God's side." Though Lincoln's remark is just that, a remark and not a prayer, it reveals the attitude and thought underpinning our view that prayer functions to determine what should be an individual's wishes. Lincoln's remark, not the general's, clearly indicates that he questioned his own will and perspective, his wish for victory. The remark reflects a struggle to determine God's will and what should be desired above all.

The concept "God's will" troubles the skeptic, and rightly so. But it should be remembered that from a mature religious perspective God's will is never apprehended directly,. The example of Lincoln bears this out. From a mature religious perspective, God's will is not a definite "yes" or "no" but rather a "could be." There are limiting cases where we can say that a certain event or plan of action is not God's will, or at least if it is, then the meaning of God is destroyed (Phillips, 1981).

In the best of circumstances, then, God's will is always an interpretation made in the context of a religious community or tradition. There are checks against arbitrary assertions that one knows God's will. There are standards for listening properly, for knowing when one has a better grasp of God's will.

But how does mature prayer accomplish the goal of facing this other reality? It does so by becoming a unique form of dialogue. Prayer may begin as talking *at* a God out there in a specific location, a God who intervenes directly to do our will if we have been good (Oser, 1988), a God perhaps valued and even loved but not a God to whom we "listen." However, with development, prayer becomes a talking *with* rather than at God. Something seems to come back: a thought, a feeling, a newly apprehended truth, insight, or directive rather than a direct divine action.

Mature prayer also functions to help change the way the self feels. But it does so in a very different way than described by Freud. Freud's description is of a child seeking comfort in the arms of a nurturing and protective adult. In contrast, the description we have in mind is of an adult seeking the comfort and support of what is felt to be companionship with God in order to be strong, hopeful, and loving when facing reality, even when tempted to be weak, despairing, and hateful. In short, there is real work in this kind of prayer, not the work of denial but rather the work of coping with and getting beyond feelings that harm others or ourselves. James (1902, p. 474) alludes to both the process and the effects of such prayer in the following comments: "The belief is not that particular events are tempered more towardly to us by a superintending providence, as a reward for our reliance, but that by cultivating the continuous sense of our connection with the power that made things as they are, we are tempered more towardly for their reception. The outward face of nature need not alter, but the expressions of meaning in it alter. It was dead and is alive again. . . . We meet a new world when we meet the old world in the spirit which this kind of prayer infuses."

The third positive function served by mature prayer is to enhance a feeling of "presence," to foster an experience of closeness to or even union with God, for its own sake. Our Western tradition has overemphasized the dogmatic element in religion; dogma is only a part of religion, perhaps even a minor part. Faith is not to be equated with belief. At the heart of the religious life is not so much dogma as what James (1902, p. 474) called a vivid sense of the "reality of the unseen." One arrives at this sense not so much through rational or even irrational thinking as though acting, prayer, and ritual. In Fosdick's (1931, p. 36) words, "Only to one who prays can God make himself vivid. . . . Men say that they do not pray because to them God is not real, but a truer statement generally would be that God is not real because they do not pray. Granted a belief that God is, the practice of prayer is necessary to make God not merely an idea held in the mind but a Presence recognized in the life."

The most obvious examples of how prayer functions as a conduit to the experience of God are the so-called wordless prayers in the contemplative tradition and the ritual prayers such as the Rosary. But even in the most ordinary spontaneous prayers one can detect a struggle to become closer to God, especially when those prayers make intimate thoughts and feelings known to God.

To summarize, prayer begins as an effort to bend God to our will. It functions first and foremost to change the reality outside of ourselves. It begins as a talking *at* rather than *with* God. But with age and development prayer becomes a way to discover and mold ourselves to what is felt to be God's will, to feel connected to God in order to cope with or change troublesome feelings, and to experience closeness to or even union with God for its own sake.

Explaining Prayer's Development

So far we have defined the development of prayer in terms of shifts in prayer's functions, shifts that often occur with age. We need now to explain just why or how these shifts occur. We focus here on "internal," "inside-out" explanations, that is, explanations in terms of changes going on inside individuals who pray. However, we pursue these explanations with the understanding that the internal changes rest on the "outside-in" processes described so insightfully by Kaye (1982), Vygotsky (Wertsch, 1985), and others. We take it as a given, then, that mature prayer develops out of years of social interaction allowing individuals to understand what it means to be a self in intimate dialogue with another. The only outside-in explanations we flatly reject are those that treat prayer as something learned through imitation and reinforcement.

We have defined mature prayer as a dialogue functioning in an individual's search for the right wishes, to get beyond troublesome feelings, and to feel close to God. So, our explanations of prayer are framed here in terms of the capacities underlying the kind of dialogue and the kind of searching, coping, and closeness that we find in mature prayer. The explanations are of three general types: psychoanalytic-object relations, cognitive-developmental, and religious-structural.

Psychoanalytic-Object Relations Explanations. Following Winnicott (1986) and Rizzuto (1979), prayer develops because it is a transitional phenomenon and because images of God change. As a transitional phenomenon where the boundaries between subjective and objective are blurred, prayer provides space and freedom to create, fantasize, and play with thoughts and feelings. This space and freedom occur because of, not in spite of, the problem of determining God's existence and whether prayer is talking to oneself or to God. If God were a tangible other or clearly a fantasized other, there would not be the kind of serious play or groping that one finds in prayer and that supports or pushes development.

Prayer also develops because images of self and others develop. Prayer to discover God's will, prayer for changes in feelings, prayer to become closer to God, such prayer presumes an autonomous, responsible self and a God who is more partner and friend than parent.

Cognitive-Developmental Explanations. Psychoanalysis is not the only perspective that focuses on understandings of self and others. Cognitive-developmentalists such as Piaget (1954), Elkind (1967), and Kohlberg and Gilligan (1971) have long focused on self-other differentiation as a starting point for cognitive development. So, a cognitive-developmental explanation of prayer's development in general and development in adolescence in particular might entail the following sequence:

At first, self and other are taken for granted as separate, real, and related. God is at once overdifferentiated from the self (being all-powerful, all-loving, and so on) and underdifferentiated (being in basic agreement with the self's will and perspective). With adolescence comes an appreciation that thoughts and feelings are creations of the self, an inner self not always directly visible to others. This new appreciation for one's own subjectivity and that of others creates doubt in the validity/acceptability of one's inner self as well as doubt in the true nature of others. From this point of view, then, the act of praying for the right wishes and for different feelings reflects a developing capacity to appreciate the inner self and the difficulty of truly knowing another. And the loneliness that comes from feeling the distance between the inner (hidden) selves of self and others explains the motive to pray in terms of a need to feel close to God.

Vygotsky's (1976) "zone of proximal development" provides the cognitive-developmental equivalent of a transitional phenomenon. With Vygotsky's concept, development in prayer can be explained as individuals examining and transforming wishes and feelings through discovery or construction of *new meanings* that satisfy them and that help them adapt. Just as play is the preschooler's zone to practice moving beyond perceptual givens when attributing meaning to objects, so too prayer is the adolescent's zone to practice moving beyond the givens of immediate wishes and immediate reactions to life's predicaments in a search for new meanings. If, for example, death is at first a terrible and final end, in prayer it can become a homecoming, horizon, or temporary sleep. Prayer develops, then, as a search for and construction of new and better meanings that effect more satisfying wishes and plans.

Religious-Structural Explanations. Prayer's development also depends on development of general religious thought structures, in particular, on achievement of at least Stage 4 in the models of Fowler and Oser. Fowler's (1981) Stage 4 describes movement away from conventional views of religion and conventional value systems and the emergence of an "executive ego," which is a view of development similar to that of Erikson and Kohlberg. From this viewpoint, development brings a relocation of authority, from outside to inside the self. This relocation seems at first to suggest an abandonment of principles and shared values, but it in fact brings the opposite. For what are abandoned are not principles and values but rather slavish devotion to external religious perspectives without regard to circumstance. The Lincoln example helps to illustrate Fowler's point: A mind that critically judges the perspectives of both self and other, a mind that searches continuously for the "right" way or a way that brings one closer to an ideal, is a mind engaged in the kind of searching prayer described earlier.

So too, Oser (1988, p. 3) finds development of autonomy in the development of religious judgment concurrent with a subordination of self to something felt to transcend the self, as evident in the following description of his Stage 4:

> Lack of a notion of an Ultimate Being (God) intervening directly in this world; rather there is a concept of a divine plan which ultimately makes all things meaningful; interpretation of life events as linked to an ultimate force which eventually stands behind the free spirit and the autonomous rationality of man; trust that in the long run there will be a solution of every problem, though not necessarily in the way we wish initially, because the transcendence of God informs all of man's immanent doing in this world.

Individuals who have reached Oser's Stage 4, then, take responsibility for their actions, while realizing that actual solutions to life's problems are often very different from those imagined in first wishes. So too, mature prayer can be characterized as acceptance of responsibility for searching and as openness to answers that surprise.

With these understandings of why and how prayer develops we can turn now to a study conducted to both elaborate on and lend empirical support to our model.

The Study of Prayer Development

Our study was designed to show developments during adolescence in prayer's functions and meaning, as evidenced both by the way adolescents pray and by the way they speak about prayer.

Sample Population. We would have done best had we been able to sample spontaneous prayers from adolescents of all backgrounds. But such an ambitious project was not feasible. We chose instead to focus on solicited prayers and answers to questions about prayer among eighty-nine middle-class adolescents and young adults from Catholic schools. Almost all of these respondents reported that they prayed frequently and shared their families' and churches' commitment to the Catholic faith. About equal numbers of males and females were represented, drawn from the seventh and ninth grades of junior high and high schools and from a college undergraduate psychology class.

Although the population range of our sample was narrow, the solicited prayers and answers to questions about prayer did not seem sectarian in obvious or even subtle ways. Therefore, we think our findings generalize to a much larger and more diverse sample of adolescents, at least to those who pray.

Solicited Prayers. In previous studies of prayer, the focus has been almost exclusively on the question of prayer's meaning as communicated in interviews about prayer. But interviews reveal only part of what prayer means to individuals.

Method: Data Collection and Response Typology. To capture the inner dynamic of prayer, to reveal just how prayer functions in the lives of individuals, we chose to look at prayers solicited in reference to situations calling for prayer.

We asked subjects to write prayers for six hypothetical situations, situations any adolescent would understand. The following vignette is representative:

> Karen's best friend Anne had cancer. Anne had been in the hospital over two months. The disease was getting worse. Anne was losing a lot of

weight, and her hair was starting to fall out. The doctors seemed pessimistic about her chances of recovery.

Karen managed to visit Anne at least once a week. Tonight was one of those visits. It was a Tuesday and no one else had visited Anne. This made Karen happy because it wasn't often that she and Anne had time alone together.

When visiting hours were up, Karen kissed Anne good-bye and took the elevator to the first floor. She had intended to go straight home, but when she passed the hospital chapel, she found herself stopping there to kneel in one of the pews toward the back. She felt like praying. This was her prayer:

Before evaluating the developmental status of the solicited prayers (before placing them on a vertical scale), we divided them into general types (placed them on a horizontal scale). We assumed that certain types (for example, requests, confessions) and subtypes exist at all stages, whereas other types and subtypes appear late and reveal one or more of the advanced functions discussed earlier here. Furthermore, we assumed that the question of a prayer's developmental status might be answered by noting subtle variations in content and not simply by noting its type.

We divided prayers into the following general types: (1) requests, (2) confessions, (3) thanksgivings, and (4) expressions of thoughts, feelings, and questioning. We assumed that prayers in this last category would appear late since they indicate most clearly a struggle to find meaning, to cope with feelings, and, in many cases, to feel closer to God. An example is the following response to the above example: "I don't know why it is Anne who is dying. It seems so unfair. She's so good."

In addition, we divided requests within prayers into subtypes based on the nature of the requested changes: (1) in objective reality, that is, tangible reality "outside" the self ("Make Anne get well"), (2) in subjective reality, that is, reality "inside" the self ("Give me strength to help Anne"), and (3) in spiritual reality, that is, reality felt to be outside the self but not tangible ("If Anne dies, let her go to heaven," heaven being an example of spiritual reality). We assumed prayers for changes in subjective reality would appear late because they clearly function as a means of coping with or changing feelings. Finally, these general types of requests were further subdivided into categories based on content, for example, requests for change in the subjective reality of another ("Help Anne to feel loved even during this difficult time," a case of using prayer to change feelings in another).

Confessions within prayers were divided into two general categories: those that simply stated the nature of some transgression and those that went on to explain the meaning of the transgression (why what was done, thought, or said was wrong). We construed explanations within confessions as signs of prayer functioning to foster understanding (in oneself) of a better wish or will than the wish or will that motivated the transgression in the first place.

The term *prayer* here refers to any unit within a response that fell into one of the above categories. A response to any of the six hypothetical situations could thus encompass one, two, or several prayers. Interjudge agreement, based on scoring of one-third of the sample of prayers from written instructions, was 76 percent.

Results: Qualitative Analyses of Responses. Age-related changes in prayers were found in our study. Owing to space limitations here, we can present only an illustrative sample of responses to the vignettes used to solicit prayers. Again, the story of Karen and Anne is representative.

The seventh graders were direct in requesting that the dying friend get well. There was no sense of searching for the right wish, wrestling with feelings, or trying to overcome distance between themselves and God. The following prayer was typical of this age group: "God, please, in the name of Jesus, help my friend Anne to get better. If this is impossible, please take care of her in heaven. Amen."

The ninth graders also prayed in order to request something, however, for the boys the requests more often had to do with changes in feelings, usually the feelings of others. Here is a prayer typical of a ninth-grade boy: "Lord, please grant my friend Anne the strength and courage to overcome her problem. Please send some optimism upon her spirit so she can continue to be herself. Also, please help her cancer be treated in a way that will help her overcome death. She is my best friend. From this experience I have grown in a more loving way. So please help her. Give her strength and guidance."

In contrast, the undergraduates' prayers showed definite signs of searching, struggling, and doubting. In examining their prayers, one can sense their considerable effort to understand and communicate feelings as well as to question old ways of wishing and thinking about God. The result is a more intimate praying, or at least a praying that seems more intent on revealing the self, as one might do in dialogue with a friend. Here is one example:

I'm not really sure why I'm here God. I guess I just needed to talk to someone and pray. I'm here for two reasons. One is to make Anne and myself strong. I hope we both can deal with this. I'm starting to find it hard because I feel like I'm losing her, so could you please give us the courage and strength to make it through this no matter what happens? The other thing is I want to thank you. You've given me a great friend, and I know at times I get angry at you because of Anne's sickness, but I'm just talking out my frustration. I'm sorry. Thanks once again. I've told Anne how much she's meant to me, and, well, I just wanted to thank you. Also one more thing; could you help her family and friends be strong too? Let them know right now they still have Anne, not to act like she's already dead. She's alive. Thanks.

In the following example, the struggle to find meaning is even more clear: "God, Why? Why do you choose certain people to remain healthy and others to become ill? I realize you have a purpose for everything, so please don't make Anne suffer. I don't know what life would be without her, and if she will be more comfortable in Heaven with you, then I guess it is meant to be. Please guide Anne and her family, and most of all please don't let her suffer anymore."

With one exception, the prayer situations elicited mostly requests. That one exception put subjects in the situation of praying after they had been critical of a friend, "Isabel," behind her back. The younger subjects simply apologized, as in the following example: "Dear God, I'm sorry about all those bad things I said about Isabel. Please forgive me." However, the undergraduates went much further, drawing out just why being critical behind a friend's back is wrong, as in this example: "Dear God, I realize what I just did, and I pray that you could give me strength not to fault people and to not be influenced by my other friends into stabbing people in the back. In the midst of wanting to be "Miss Popular" I judge people without even being in their shoes. This is something I pray you could help me with. Amen." Here, then, we see prayer used to sort out wishes and adopt the better; the wish to be popular is subordinated to the wish to be a caring friend who does not judge.

Results: Statistical Analyses. Where appropriate, both chi-square analyses and analyses of variance, 3 (age) by 2 (sex), were computed on percentage scores, for example, percentage of prayers that were requests. The results of statistical analyses on solicited prayers indicated a shift during adolescence away from using prayer to request changes in objective reality and toward using prayer to change or cope with feelings and increase intimacy with God. This shift was indicated most clearly by significant increases with age in the percentage of prayers that were simply expressions of thoughts, feelings, and questions and by significant increases in the percentage that were requests for changes in another's feelings. There were also significant increases with age in the percentage of confessions providing explanations of wrongdoing.

The results did not provide overwhelming evidence for a shift toward using prayer to search for and adopt "better" wishes ("God's will"). However, as the examples demonstrate, there definitely seemed to be a struggle among the older subjects to determine the meaning of situations. This kind of a struggle seems to be a prerequisite to using prayer to discover or reaffirm better wishes, since a struggle to determine meaning suggests that old views (old assumptions about what is to be wished for) are being questioned.

Questions About Prayer. After constructing prayers to the six hypothetical situations, subjects were asked to answer the following questions about prayer: (1) What are prayers for? (2) Does it make sense to pray for miracles? (3) How do you know when a prayer is answered? (4) Why don't some prayers seem to get answered? The first two questions were intended to test subjects' beliefs about the function(s) of prayer. We expected only the older subjects to show signs of appreciating the mature functions of prayer. The second two questions were intended to test subjects' epistemology concerning prayer. We expected only the older subjects to show a clear appreciation of the subjective nature of prayer, an appreciation that underlies the use of prayer to focus on feelings and alternative wishes.

Response Typology. Responses to the first question were divided according to whether reference was made to (1) prayer's surface functions (for example, thanking God, talking to God), (2) the underlying function of changing or coping with feelings (for example, asking for strength), (3) the underlying function of becoming closer to God, or (4) the underlying function of searching for and discovering God's will. Responses to the second question were divided between those focusing on whether or not miracles happen ("It makes sense because miracles happen") and those focusing on the changes such prayer can have on feelings and attitudes ("Praying for miracles gives us hope").

Responses to the third question were grouped according to whether reference was made to (1) changes in objective reality ("When a request is granted," suggesting you can see the results), (2) changes in subjective reality ("You feel differently"), or (3) the uncertainty involved and the need for interpretation to determine when a prayer has been answered ("It's hard to be sure"). And responses to the fourth question were categorized on the basis of whether explanations were in terms of (1) God's will or "mystery," (2) something wrong with the prayer, the person praying, or God, or (3) the appearance versus reality distinction and the problem of interpreting when a prayer is answered ("Sometimes a prayer doesn't seem to get answered because the answer isn't what we wanted or expected"), evidence for distinguishing between one's immediate wish or will and a deeper wish or will that one can accept when recognized.

Interjudge agreement, based on scoring of one-third of the responses to questions about prayer from written instructions, was 82 percent.

Results. The responses to the four questions about prayer provided clear evidence for the expected age changes in how adolescents view the function of prayer. Responses to the first question showed a definite shift away from referring to surface functions (to give thanks, to ask for things) and toward referring to the underlying functions of changing or coping with feelings and, eventually, of becoming closer to God. However, none of the groups referred to prayer as functioning to search for or discover God's will.

Responses to the second question indicated that most subjects felt praying for miracles does make sense, but there were age-related differences in the reasons offered. Almost all of the younger subjects said it makes sense because "miracles happen." In contrast, the majority of ninth graders and undergraduates said praying for miracles provides hope or some other positive change in feeling or attitude.

Responses to the third question showed a definite shift away from reliance on tangible results to reliance on feelings, and then to reliance on interpretations open to question: Over 66 percent of the seventh graders said something like "When a request is granted," as if the results of praying are objective facts that do not require interpretation. Fifty percent of the ninth graders and 28 percent of the undergraduates gave responses similar to those of the seventh graders, but 31 percent of the ninth graders and 20 percent of the undergraduates gave "change in feelings" as the symptom of a prayer being answered, and 19 percent of the ninth graders and 52 percent of the undergraduates said that it is hard to be sure.

Finally, responses to the fourth question showed an expected shift with age: The seventh graders either responded by simple reference to "God's will" or by reference to something wrong with the prayer or person praying. Ninth graders also referred to something wrong with the prayer or person praying, but many explicitly referred to the problem of interpreting when a prayer is answered and how a prayer might be answered, though in a different way than what is expected. For the undergraduates, the majority referred to the distinction of appearance (of a prayer not being answered) versus reality (answered in an unexpected way). The results on this question, then, provide clear evidence that with age (and development) there is an appreciation that prayers function in the discovery and adoption of "better" wishes.

Conclusion

Our study of prayer reaffirms the explanations of religious development and prayer outlined earlier. In the solicited prayers, we see clearly how prayer is experienced as talk to a unique other (God), a transitional phenomenon and zone for discovering meaning that develops with changes in the way God is imaged. In both the solicited prayers and the responses to the questions about prayer, we see prayer developing out of adolescents' discovery of their own subjectivity and that of others (see Long, Elkind, and Spilka, 1967; Kohlberg and Gilligan, 1971). The seventh graders provided examples of a naive faith not only in a God "out there" but also in a self "out there" and visible to all. But the ninth graders and especially the undergraduates shifted the focus to the inner world of feelings and to an awareness of how difficult it is to know what is true and best. We are reminded of Rosenberg's (1989, p. 34) conclusion after analyzing adolescents' responses to questions about prayers' efficacy: "What sets (older adolescents) . . . apart . . . clearly is the adolescents' valuation of prayer as important in itself and as having a great effect on the praying person himself." Also, in both the solicited prayers and the responses to questions about prayer we see the emergence of the kind of active, autonomous self relating to his or her God that has been described so well by Oser (1988) and Fowler (1981).

Our study of prayer has, then, reaffirmed our belief in the usefulness of a developmental perspective on prayer as a way to understand the phenomenon. However, these results are simply a beginning. There is a need to follow the development of prayer throughout the life cycle. There is a need to look at the conditions fostering or inhibiting prayer's development. There is a need for empirical research that links prayer to general cognitive and emotional stages, as well as to more specific religious stages of thinking and feeling.

There also is a need to raise and answer questions about the effects that situation, culture, and institutional affiliation have on prayer. By ignoring questions of context, we may have unintentionally prejudiced the evaluation of prayers. Our model has indicated that with age new functions are added to old. However, this model can imply that certain prayers are "better" than others. We caution against using the term "better" to distinguish one type of prayer from another. An evaluation of prayer, as distinct from an explanation of prayer's development, cannot be made without regard for context. After all, what parent of a dying child would be thought childish, primitive, or immature simply for repeating "Save my child"?

In sum, more research is needed to do justice to the complexities and significance of this private, oft-ignored, but pervasive exercise of feeling, thought, and faith. Prayer not only reveals the heart of religion, it also reveals the heart of the individual. It reveals the individual's struggle to be growing, happy, and good. And it reveals the self evolving into what Stern (1985) referred to as a "shared self," a self neither alone nor fused but rather separate and related.

References

Elkind, D. "Egocentrism in Adolescence." *Child Development,* 1967, *38*, 1025–1034.

Fosdick, H. E. *The Meaning of Prayer.* New York: Association Press, 1931.

Fowler, J. W. *Stages of Faith: The Psychology of Human Development and the Quest for Meaning.* New York: Harper & Row, 1981.

Freud, S. *The Future of an Illusion.* Garden City, N.Y.: Anchor Books, 1964. (Originally published 1927.)

James, W. *The Varieties of Religious Experience.* New York: Longmans, Green, 1902.

Kaye, K. *The Mental and Social Life of Babies.* Chicago: University of Chicago Press, 1982.

Kohlberg, L., and Gilligan, C. "The Adolescent as a Philosopher: The Discovery of the Self in a Postconventional World." *Daedalus,* 1971, *100*, 1051–1086.

Long, D., Elkind, D., and Spilka, B. "The Child's Conception of Prayer." *Journal for the Scientific Study of Religion,* 1967, *6*, 101–109.

Oser, F. K. "Genese und Logik der Entwicklung des religiösen Bewuesstseins: Eine Entgegnung auf Kritiken" [Toward a logic of religious judgment: A reply to my critics]. In K. E. Nipkow, F. Schweitzer, and J. W. Fowler (eds.), *Glaubensentwicklung und Erziehung*. Gütersloh, Germany: Gerd Mohn, 1988. English translation in J. W. Fowler, K. E. Nipkow, and F. Schweitzer (eds.), *Stages of Faith and Religious Development: An Intercontinental Debate*. New York: Crossroads, 1991.

Phillips, D. Z. *The Concept of Prayer*. New York: Seabury, 1981.

Piaget, J. *The Construction of Reality in the Child*. New York: Basic Books, 1954.

Rizzuto, A.-M. *The Birth of the Living God: A Psychoanalytic Study*. Chicago: University of Chicago Press, 1979.

Rosenberg, R. "The Development of the Concept of Prayer in Jewish Israeli Children and Adolescents." Unpublished manuscript, Department of Psychology, Hebrew University, Jerusalem, 1989.

Stern, D. *The Interpersonal World of the Infant*. New York: Basic Books, 1985.

Vygotsky, L. "Play and Its Role in the Mental Development of the Child." In J. Bruner, A. Jolly, and K. Sylva (eds.), *Play: Its Role in Development and Evolution*. New York: Basic Books, 1976.

Wertsch, J. *Vygotsky*. Cambridge, Mass.: Harvard University Press, 1985.

Winnicott, D. W. *Playing and Reality*. New York: Tavistock, 1986.

W. George Scarlett is assistant professor of child study in the Department of Child Study, Tufts University, Medford, Massachusetts.

Lucy Perriello is a research assistant at the University of Massachusetts Medical Center, Worcester, Massachusetts.

Complementarity reasoning helps dissolve perceived contradictions
that otherwise might adversely affect religious development.

The Role of Complementarity Reasoning in Religious Development

K. Helmut Reich

Religion has been criticized for involving a logic of absurdity full of unresolvable contradictions, such as the following: (1) According to the Bible, God created the complete universe and all it contains in six days. From a scientific perspective the universe, though finite in age, may never have had a beginning as such. Human beings have in all likelihood emerged from other forms of animal life as the result of a long evolution, which also has brought about human self-consciousness. (2) Bad things happen to good and innocent people, such as when a child dies of cancer and when hundreds perish in an earthquake or a flood. Yet God is said to be all-powerful, just, and loving. (3) The Chalcedonian Definition (A.D. 451) states that Jesus Christ is "truly God and truly man" and "is known in two natures [which exist] without confusion, without change, without division, without separation." Here are two illustrations of what religious contradiction means in people's lives: Corinne (twelve years old) said in an interview, "At school I have learned that the world came into its own with a big bang, and in religion they tell you that God created it. I just don't know what to make of it." When Helen learned from her doctor that she had multiple sclerosis and what that would entail until she died, totally diminished as a

The author thanks the editors and reviewers of the following journals for their help in clarifying some of the views reported in this chapter: *Human Development, Journal of Psychology and Theology,* and *Zygon: Journal of Religion & Science.* The editor of the *Journal of Psychology and Theology* kindly permitted the use of copyrighted material. Part of the work reported was done in collaboration with Anton A. Bucher, Reto L. Fetz, Fritz K. Oser, and Peter Valentin.

human person, she broke down and cried, "Why should this happen to me? I've tried to be a good person. I have a husband and young children who need me. I don't deserve this. Why should God make me suffer like this?" (Kushner, 1983, p. 15).

Faced with these perceived contradictions, individuals have four options. They can (1) accept contradictions as typical of religious life (for example, "the mystery of Christ is beyond human grasp"), (2) jettison whatever seems "illogical," thereby limiting religion as we know it (for example, "the story about Adam and Eve simply shows that people did not know any better at the time it was written; so it is an unimportant detail we can best forget"), (3) "explain away" any perceived contradiction (for example, "God sends us these tragedies to test our faith and make us grow"), or (4) explicate rationally why particular perceived contradictions are only apparent (for example, "just as we are humans because our life involves a body and a mind, the life of Christ Jesus involves his godhead and his humanity; therefore, he can deeply and fully communicate with both God Father and human beings"). This chapter deals with the fourth option and the use of complementarity reasoning both to resolve perceived contradictions and paradoxes and to show their usefulness for conveying deeper meaning. The discussion that follows defines this type of reasoning and outlines how it functions, develops, and relates to other types of reasoning.

Nature and Function of Complementarity Reasoning

The expression "thinking in terms of complementarity" (Oser and Reich, 1987) here means coordinating "noncompatible" (neither compatible nor incompatible) theories or belief systems in such a way that they illuminate and limit each other when describing or explaining the same reference object or state of affairs. That is, complementarity reasoning can make sense of perceived contradictions or paradoxes, so that the use of this type of reasoning produces better-founded results than other types of reasoning. For instance, when asked how she sees the creation versus evolution problem, Renate (twenty years old) said, "The possibility of evolution was contained in God's 'kick-off' at the origin . . . but God probably did not interfere with evolution itself . . . and perhaps so far not all of the initial potential has yet come to fruition."

Clearly, the use of complementarity reasoning is not called for in the simple situations of everyday life that require a yes-no or a better-worse decision. Rather, this type of reasoning is suitable for certain complex situations and certain kinds of problems involving apparent contradictions or paradoxes. Kaiser (1976, pp. 43–47) describes eleven characteristics of the kinds of problems that lend themselves to complementarity reasoning. For example, something or someone appears in at least two different modes (such as the divinity and humanity of Jesus Christ), and the whole is characterized by a unity of being (despite the distinctness of the modes). In each mode the explanation is "complete," but of necessity not exhaustive; all modes together make up the phenomenon in question; neither mode is reducible to the other, nor derivable from the other. The modes are linked internally; one mode appears "weakly" in the other (as when Jesus is free from sin, in Heb. 4:15). Under a given set of circumstances one mode may be recognized clearly but not the other. Additional problem distinctions are discussed elsewhere (for example, Russell, 1989; Reich, 1990b).

Given the kinds of problems described above, complementarity reasoning serves as a heuristic, a useful device for getting to a genuine understanding. It does this by (Reich, 1990c) (1) clarifying and defining the phenomenon to be described or explained, (2) listing all descriptions and explanations A, B, C, . . . from different categories, even if they are considered incompatible, incommensurable, and so on by the ambient culture, and possibly adding new ones and dealing with any conflicts arising, (3) establishing under which circumstances A (B, C, . . .) describes or explains particular aspects of the phenomenon, and, in case a genuine understanding does not come forth, reconsidering A (B, C, . . .) as an approximation or even only as an analogy, (4) discovering and describing any (unexpected) links between the different descriptions or explanations, in particular, bringing out (unsuspected) common attributes and coinherences, (5) assessing to what extent the relative (proportional) explanatory contribution of each mode depends on the current strength of the other mode(s) (as distinct from a contribution described by a fixed relationship), (6) working out an overarching synopsis or theory that explains the various features of the reference object or state of affairs with regard to different circumstances and situations, and (7) explaining any shifts in meaning of the concepts needed to explain the phenomenon, its modes, and the new synopsis or theory. With this range of analytic and heuristic power complementarity reasoning often leads to conjoint lines of explanations that were previously thought to be either conflicting (calling for the elimination of one) or irrelevant with respect to each other.

To apply complementarity reasoning to problems like the first two introduced above, it is important to be aware of a possible inverse result: In certain cases such reasoning leads to a separation of lines of description and explanation that were previously confounded. An example from physics is the causal explanation of a certain event and its spatiotemporal description. In a game of billiards, a player will most naturally (and rightly) causally link the force and direction he or she has imparted to the cue with the ensuing movement(s) of the ball(s). In contrast, a physicist who "plays a game of billiards" with (sub)atomic particles cannot argue that way. Applying complementarity reasoning, he or she can reason either in terms of causality (which in the applicable quantum physics only allows *probabilistic* predictions for inherent reasons, that is, not reasons of his or her ignorance) or in terms of a description of a given interaction-with-the-physical-world, but the two cannot be linked in detail as in the case of the billiards player. A corresponding example in theology is the mutual exclusiveness (but complementarity) of discussing a theologically relevant event in a causal mode of explanation that involves God's action in the world versus in a personal and historical mode of description (Russell, 1989). Some of the perceived contradictions we are examining arise because the causal and personal modes are collapsed, as when discussing a game of billiards with hard balls instead of keeping them separate as required by complementarity reasoning. At this point, it is useful to go deeper into the examples of complementarity reasoning and show how it works.

Complementarity Reasoning and the Problem of Suffering. How can there be a powerful, just, and loving God if innocent children are suffering from and dying of cancer? Although there is no single, conclusive, entirely satisfactory answer, there are, Vieth (1988, p. 25) suggests, at least four *possible* answers to this question. We can (1) reject or redefine God's power (introducing Satan, natural forces, original sin, God's self-limitations, and so on), (2) reject or redefine the goodness of God (for instance, by arguing that God tests us, makes us grow through pain), (3) redefine evil (for instance, by perceiving it as contributing to a larger harmony), or (4) give up (by reasoning that God simply does not exist, or that what happened is a mystery beyond human comprehension). Of course, people do not live on logical possibilities. Hence, in practice, even if eventually one of the answers is found acceptable, it may take much working through—in effect, a transformation of psychic state—to get there, as in the case of Helen quoted earlier.

How can complementarity reasoning help? As already indicated, such reasoning suggests that we keep a causal explanation involving God's action in the world separate from a personal and historical description of what happened. In other words, the basic *theological* assumption is that God's action cannot be merged point-by-point with diachronic event description into a unified picture (Russell, 1989). Both modes are irreducible to each other, although both are necessary for a complete understanding. In the causal mode evil may be explained in terms of, say, divine self-limitation or defective secondary causality, but a detailed, factual interpretation is not admitted. Whereas in the personal mode the actual historical events are described without a causal explanation. Perhaps we can take a cue from Jesus dying on the cross: "My God, my God, why hast thou forsaken me" (Matt. 27:46). Although suffering almost unbearably, Jesus stays in the descriptive mode of his near-despair without merging it with a causal mode. In particular, he does not accuse God of being the cause of his agonizing. Or take Rabbi Kushner's ([1981] 1983, pp. 84–85) belief about Auschwitz: "Where was God? I have to believe with Dorothee Sölle that He was with the victims, and not with the murderers, but having given man freedom to choose, including the freedom to choose to hurt his neighbor, there was nothing God could do to prevent it."

Before somebody objects that confounding of both modes does occur in the Bible, let me elaborate. Indeed, in Gen. 50:20, Joseph links God's interaction-with-the-world and his life tapestry when speaking to his brothers: "But as for you, ye thought evil against me; but God meant it unto good, to bring to pass, as it is this day, to save much people alive." Or take Job speaking to God, "Thou art become cruel to me: with thy strong hand thou opposest thyself against me. Thou liftest me up to the wind; thou causest me to ride upon it, and dissolvest my substance" (Job 30:21–22). So what is the difference? The point is that both Joseph and Job do the linking in general, overall terms and not in a step-by-step manner. (In quantum physics this corresponds to discussing particle lifetimes in terms of average values, although in any particular decay a precise prediction is impossible in principle.)

Furthermore, complementarity reasoning emphasizes the situation specificity, the dependence on circumstances of the visibility of the various modes of God's being and of the sufferer's being, as distinct from assuming fixed characteristics that hold throughout. Depending on the situation, (1) God is understood as being powerful (for example, in the testimonies of Joseph and Job quoted above) or as suffering with the being(s) concerned ("Likewise the Spirit also helpeth our infirmities: for we know not what we should pray for as we ought: but the Spirit itself maketh intercession for us with groanings which cannot be uttered" [Rom. 8:26]), (2) the sense of human life is attributed preponderantly to involvement on Earth, the temporal dimension (for example, Jesus's teaching that "Ye are the salt of the earth: but if the salt has lost his savour, wherewith shall it be salted? It is henceforth good for nothing, but to be cast out, and to be trodden under foot of men" [Matt. 5:13]), or to involvement in heaven, the eternal dimension (for example, "For I reckon that the sufferings of this present time are not worthy of comparison with the glory that shall be revealed in us" [Rom. 8:18]), or (3) the facts are stressed as they were experienced in the past, or the accent is put on any ensuing developments, or differing interpretations, that the future may bring (for example, "For now, we see through a glass darkly; but then, face to face: now I know in part; but then shall I know even as also I am known" [1 Cor. 13:12]).

Complementarity Reasoning and the Chalcedonian Definition. How are we to understand the statement that "Jesus Christ . . . is known in two natures [which exist] . . . without division, without separation"? One plausible explanation is that the statement has no deep meaning since it was made as a result of political pressure before and during the Council of Chalcedon. However, there is evidence that at least some council fathers thought in terms of complementarity when phrasing the definition so as to describe the mystery of Jesus Christ in the best terms possible at the time (Reich, 1990b).

Using complementarity reasoning, the perceived paradox disappears when it is seen that circumstances codetermine which nature (divine or human) is more clearly visible. Thus, the divine rather than the human becomes clear in the passage "Verily, verily, I say unto you, before Abraham was, I am" (John 8:58), whereas the human is emphasized in the passage describing Jesus' death: "Jesus, when he had cried again, yielded up the ghost" (Matt. 27:50). (For a discussion of the more subtle aspects of complementarity reasoning used to decipher meaning from the Chalcedonian Definition, see Reich, 1990b.) But even with this abbreviated discussion it is clear that the perceived paradox in the statement about the two natures of Jesus is not swept under the carpet, as would have been the easy option if politics were the overriding force. The process of complementarity reasoning allows us to see the paradox as both apparent and productive for conveying a particular meaning and understanding of Jesus: His two natures are neither compatible (in which case they could *both* be perceived clearly *all of the time*) nor incompatible (meaning that he is *either* divine *or* human, all of the time), but rather noncompatible, that is, a given nature appears clearly under given circumstances (Reich, 1989b).

Similarly, in regard to the concept of the Trinity, we can understand that the statement "in the name of the Father, and of the Son, and of the Holy Ghost" (Matt. 28:19) refers to a *single* God. The three modes appear most clearly under different circumstances: (1) "Our Father . . . Give us this day our daily bread. And forgive us our debt, as we forgive our debtors. And lead us not into temptation, but deliver us from evil" (Matt. 6:9–13; see also Luke 11:23–4); (2) "Neither knoweth any man the Father, save the Son, and he to whomsoever the Son will reveal him (Matt. 11:27); and (3) "Because the love of God is shed abroad in our hearts by the Holy Ghost which is given to us" (Rom. 5:5). Again, the purpose of complementarity reasoning is not to explain away apparent paradoxes but rather to show their usefulness for providing deeper understanding in particular situations and under particular circumstances. Here, the appearance of three distinct modes when referring to God avoids the danger of using so many predicates that God appears strange and remote.

Complementarity Reasoning and Ontogenesis

By now, it should be clear that complementarity reasoning is no simple thought process and that it emerges in fully developed form relatively late in life, if at all. However, children and adolescents do respond, in varying ways, to the same problems resolved through complementarity reasoning. To describe the developmental level of responses to problems calling for complementarity reasoning, Oser and Reich (1987, p. 182) developed the five-level model outlined in Table 1. Using Piagetian notions (Piaget and Garcia, 1983), the five levels can be characterized as follows: An individual

Table 1. Developmental Level of Responses to Situations Calling for Complementarity Reasoning to Deal with Noncompatible Explanations A and B

Level	Description
1	Explanation A and explanation B are considered separately; spontaneous judgment "true" or "false" (emphasis on alternatives, not on complementarity). Usually single-track choice of A *or* B, occasionally of both without offering a detailed justification and depending on chance, knowledge, or socialization.
2	The possibility that A *and* B may both be right is considered. A may be right, B may be right, both may be right, possibly with very different weighting factors.
3	The necessity of an explanation with the help of A as well as of B is examined. Whereas neither A nor B is generally considered correct individually, both are needed (partially).
4	Conscious connecting of A and B, explicit indication of their relation. Neither A nor B is correct (alone). The relation between A and B is analyzed (for instance "B permits the use of A" or "B cannot exist without A"). The situation-specificity of the relative contribution of A and B to the total explanation is at least intimated.
5	Construction of a generalized overarching theory (or at least synopsis), including (reconstructed/supplemented parts of) A and B and possibly an additional C. The complex mutual relationship of A and B (and C) as well as the situation-specificity of their explanatory weight is understood and incorporated into the overarching theory. Any resulting shift of meaning in the terms used is explained.

at Level 1 thinks "intra" (-categorially), at Level 2 "inter," at Level 3 "trans-intra," at Level 4 "trans-inter," and at Level 5 "trans-trans."

We tested the usefulness of this model for describing age-related changes by asking groups of children, adolescents, and young adults to respond to the question, "Who is right about the origin of the world and human beings, the Bible or the scientists?" (Reich, 1989a; compare Fetz and Oser, 1986; Fetz and Reich, 1989; Fetz, Reich, and Valentin, 1989). As expected, younger children gave Level 1 responses by siding either with the Bible or with the scientists, presumably depending on how they had been socialized. Older children more frequently gave Level 2 responses by claiming both views are somehow valid. As one child said, "I believe more in the Bible, but it is also right that humanity descended from apes."

Only during adolescence was there a conscious attempt to coordinate the various points of view. One fifteen-year-old gave this Level 3 response: "The first matter can't have appeared from nowhere. . . . A higher power, which must certainly exist, has presumably come in and somehow contrived that this matter came into being. . . . From thereon things evolved on their own . . . perhaps according to the possibilities planned by the higher power." And a young adult gave this Level 4 response: "For me there exist several models which help us to find out about the world's origin. If somebody speaks about a physics theory, in my view that does not per se contradict a religious worldview. Both are models of a beginning. [Such a model] does not represent the beginning itself, but the beginning as mirrored in human thinking. Adam and Eve in the Bible is a possible model of human origin, calling for interpretation. It was not meant really to be a scientific statement, but rather underlines the role of humanity."

In this study—involving only a small sample of children (less than one hundred subjects) with an education higher than average, between six and ten years of age—the majority were at Level 1, between eleven and fourteen years of age about one-third had reached Level 2 and another one-third Level 3, and between fifteen and twenty years of age about one-third had reached Level 4. A greater number of those older than twenty had reached Level 4. In a representative sample with persons from all walks of life, we would expect lesser percentages of Level 3 and Level 4 responses.

It should be added that there were subjects of all ages who were socialized as, or had become, agnostics or even atheists and who did not invest time or energy in answering the question. They simply stated flatly that the scientists were right or more logical.

How Is Complementarity Reasoning Related to Other Types of Reasoning?

Under this heading we consider logical, analogical, and dialectical reasoning, the first conceptually and empirically and the latter two only conceptually. Reich and Oser (1990) and Reich (1990a) hypothesize first the following developmental commonalities and differences between logical and complementarity reasoning: (1) An appropriate level of logical reasoning is a necessary but insufficient condition for reaching Levels 2-4 of complementarity reasoning. (Early) concrete-operational reasoning is necessary to reach Level 2 because both types of reasoning involve working reversibly with two dimensions. At least well-established, concrete operations (transition to formal operations) are necessary to reach Level 3 because both deal globally with (simple) systems. Finally, well-established, formal operations are necessary to reach Level 4 because both involve isolation and correlation of variables. (2) As the first hypothesis implies, not all individuals who reach a given stage of logical reasoning will reach the corresponding level of complementarity reasoning. In particular, to reach Level 4, an understanding that A and B are not independent of each other—and possibly at least an inkling that their relative contribution to the exhaustive explanation depends on the particular circumstances—is necessary.

To test these two hypotheses, my colleagues and I conducted semi-structured interviews involving three coordination tasks (nature versus nurture, to explain the performance of a concert pianist; mind versus body, to explain human functioning; and technical versus human malfunctioning, to explain a Three Mile Island– or Chernobyl-type nuclear accident) and three Piagetian tasks (snail, plant, and pendulum). The results were rated, and a logical and complementarity reasoning level was attributed to each subject. The respective numbers of intra-individual score combinations of thirty-seven subjects seven to nineteen years of age, and one subject twenty-two years of age, are shown in Table 2. To get a sense of the meaning of these combinations, consider the subjects who mastered concrete Piagetian operations (row 2 in Table 2): Their complementarity reasoning ranged from somewhat below Level 3, as expected from the first hypothesis, down to Level 1, in accord with the second hypothesis.

The corresponding values of Kendall's rank-correlation coefficient ranged from $\alpha = .466$ to $\alpha = .817$ ($p \leq .01$): Hypothesis 1 is supported. As to hypothesis 2, the interviews furnished some hints. For instance, Helene (nineteen years old) said in the mind-body interview, "When you are happy . . . the cells also fare better." She went on to explain the relative explanatory weight of theories A (the actions of the body explain behavior) and B (the actions of the mind explain behavior) in relation to driving, sleeping, and discussing. And Ottilie (twenty-two years old) insisted that she had to know the detailed situation in order to determine the respective contributions of A and B.

The relation between complementarity reasoning and analogical reasoning might best be conceived as follows: In order to apply analogical reasoning (for example, the stem of a flower, A, is like a straw for drinking, B), one first has to discover and analyze in some detail attributes and/or relations (functions) shared by A and B (Gentner, 1989; compare Bucher,

Table 2. Intra-Individual Contingency Stage Scores of Logical and Complementarity Reasoning

Level of Piagetian Operations	Level of Complementarity Reasoning									
	1	1(2)	2(1)	2	2(3)	3(2)	3	3(4)	4(3)	4
Early concrete	2									
Established concrete	2	1	1		2	1				
Transition to formal						1	2			
Early formal							8	6	2	
Established formal								3	3	4

Note: N = 38. Level 1(2) is somewhat above Level 1, Level 2(1) is somewhat below Level 2, and so on.

this volume). Similarly, to reach higher levels of complementarity reasoning, one has to bring out commonalities and differences between A and B.

The relation between complementarity reasoning and dialectical reasoning is more difficult to define (Reich, 1990c), in part because dialectical reasoning has several meanings. Most of these meanings rest on a logic that stipulates that the negation of a negation brings one back to a new situation (concept, synthesis, and so on), as opposed to bringing one back to the original starting point (as in Aristotelian logic, which applies to entities that are intrinsically situation- and time-independent). The relation, then, may rest on the fact that both complementarity and dialectical reasoning require (different) non-Aristotelian logics.

Looking at all three types of reasoning together, Secretan (1987) argues from a philosophical perspective that complementarity reasoning is situated between analogical and dialectic reasoning. The result of complementarity reasoning is neither as fixed (static) as that of analogical reasoning nor as dynamic (based on change) as that of dialectical reasoning. With complementarity reasoning, the object or state of affairs to be described or explained and the theories A and B (and C . . .) stay the same (similar to analogical reasoning). However, the respective explanatory weights of A and B (and C . . .) change, depending on (external) circumstances (similar to dialectical reasoning).

Role of Complementarity Reasoning in Advancement to Higher Levels of Religious Consciousness

So far we have looked at the role of complementarity reasoning in specific cases. Now, let us step back and look at the larger question of how complementarity reasoning fits into religious development as conceived by James Fowler, Fritz Oser, and Paul Gmünder.

When describing "Conjunctive faith and the interindividual self" (the sixth of his seven stages), Fowler (1987, p. 72) writes, "In the transition to Conjunctive faith one begins to make peace with the tension arising from the fact that truth must be approached from a number of different directions and angles of vision. As part of honoring truth, faith must maintain the tensions between these multiple perspectives and refuse to collapse them in one direction or another. . . . God is both immanent and transcendent; God is both omnipotent and a self-limiting God." Fowler clearly speaks here of complementarity reasoning. Furthermore, by emphasizing the fact that in higher stages there is a return to symbol, liturgy, and parable—all of which are "read" in multidimensional ways, Fowler (1987, p. 75) describes a phenomenon that is a product of complementarity reasoning.

Reference to complementarity reasoning is less explicit in the theory of Oser and Gmünder (1988). However, let us look at their Stage 4 (Oser, 1988, pp. 52–53): "Now an indirect, mediated relationship with an Ultimate

Being has come into existence. The individual continues to assume responsibility, but he or she wonders about the conditions for the mere possibility to carry responsibility. He or she sees his or her commitment as a way to overcome lack of meaning and hope as well as absurdity. Transcendence is now partly inside (immanence): The Ultimate Being becomes the condition for the possibility of human freedom, independence, etc., via the divine plan." The least one can say about the usefulness of complementarity reasoning in this context is that it can contribute to the coordination of ego considerations and God's plan.

Four Possible Hurdles on the Way to Complementarity Reasoning

Having established the usefulness, and even the necessity, of complementarity reasoning for religious development, an obvious question arises, "Why is this type of reasoning not used more generally?" One answer is "because of hurdles" (Reich, 1990b).

The first hurdle is lack of motivation. For a number of reasons (for example, survival value during a long evolution, preference of action over reflection, easier identity preservation), a "yes-no"-type decision comes more naturally to people than does a "both-and"-type reflection.

The second hurdle is the logic involved. Aristotle still determines what we in our Western culture construe as "logical." For many, Aristotelian logic seems as natural as eating or sleeping; and so, its absence means something is wrong or at least suspicious. Even for sophisticated critics the "nonexclusion of the middle" (tertium datur), the use of notions such as noncompatible (as opposed to compatible and incompatible), the inclusion of situation-specificity into the logic, and so on raises eyebrows.

The third hurdle may consist of adverse epistemological–philosophical beliefs such as naive realism or logical positivism, to which the founding assumptions of complementarity reasoning are unacceptable. Even a dialectic world view may be a hurdle, in that only the commonalities (not the specificity) of complementarity reasoning are perceived.

The fourth hurdle has already been discussed at some length. It can be described simply as insufficient cognitive development.

How these hurdles can be overcome in the most effective way remains to be studied. To speculate, a combination of methods developed by Kitchener and Fischer (1990), and by Lochhead and Whimbey (1987), might be particularly useful.

Conclusion

We have examined the nature of complementarity reasoning and its function for resolving the many perceived contradictions and paradoxes that characterize religious life. I have argued that complementarity reasoning is crucial to religious development. Work remains to be done on assessing the conditions under which complementarity reasoning develops, and on relating such reasoning at the highest level to other forms of thought as well as to the affective dimensions of religious development. However, I hope that the analysis of complementarity reasoning presented here makes clear that the logic in developed religious thinking is anything but absurd and does not involve logical contradictions.

References

Fetz, R. L., and Oser, F. K. "Weltbildentwicklung, moralisches und religiöses Urteil" [Development of worldviews, moral and religious judgment; on the determination of morality]. In W. Edelstein and G. Nunner-Winkler (eds.), *Zur Bestimmung der Moral*. Frankfurt, Germany: Suhrkamp, 1986.

Fetz, R. L., and Reich, K. H. "World Views and Religious Development." *Journal of Empirical Theology*, 1989, 2 (2), 46–61.

Fetz, R. L., Reich, K. H., and Valentin, P. "'Cosmogony' According to Children and Adolescents: An Empirical Study of Developmental Steps." In J. M. van der Lans and J. A. van Belzen (eds.), *Proceedings of the Fourth Symposium on the Psychology of Religion in Europe*. Nijmegen, The Netherlands: Department of Cultural Psychology and Psychology of Religion, University of Nijmegen, 1989.

Fowler, J. W. *Faith Development and Pastoral Care*. Philadelphia: Fortress Press, 1987.

Gentner, D. "The Mechanisms of Analogical Learning." In S. Vosniadou and A. Ortony (eds.), *Similarity and Analogical Reasoning*. Cambridge, England: Cambridge University Press, 1989.

Kaiser, C. B. "Christology and Complementarity." *Religious Studies*, 1976, *12*, 33–48.

Kitchener, K. S., and Fischer, K. W. "A Skill Approach to the Development of Reflective Thinking." In D. Kuhn (ed.), *Developmental Perspectives on Teaching and Learning Thinking Skills*. Vol. 21: *Contributions to Human Development*. Basel, Switzerland: Karger, 1990.

Kushner, H. S. *When Bad Things Happen to Good People*. New York: Avon, 1983. (Originally published 1981.)

Lochhead, J., and Whimbey, A. "Teaching Analytical Reasoning Through Thinking-Aloud Pair Problem Solving." In J. E. Stice (ed.), *Developing Critical Thinking and Problem-Solving Abilities*. New Directions for Teaching and Learning, no. 30. San Francisco: Jossey-Bass, 1987.

Oser, F. K. "Genese und Logik der Entwicklung des religiösen Bewuesstseins: Eine Entgegnung auf Kritiken" [Toward a logic of religious judgment: A reply to my critics]. In K. E. Nipkow, F. Schweitzer, and J. W. Fowler (eds.), *Glaubensentwicklung und Erziehung*. Gütersloh, Germany: Gerd Mohn, 1988. English translation in J. W. Fowler, K. E. Nipkow, and F. Schweitzer (eds.), *Stages of Faith and Religious Development: An Intercontinental Debate*. New York: Crossroads, 1991.

Oser, F. K., and Gmünder, P. (eds.). *Der Mensch—Stufen seiner religiösen Entwicklung. Ein strukturgenetischer Ansatz* [The human being—Stages of his or her religious development: A structural-genetic approach]. (2nd ed.) Gütersloh, Germany: Gerd Mohn, 1988. (English translation to be published by Religious Education Press, Birmingham, Ala.)

Oser, F. K., and Reich, K. H. "The Challenge of Competing Explanations: The

Development of Thinking in Terms of Complementarity of 'Theories.'" *Human Development,* 1987, *30,* 178–186.

Piaget, J., and Garcia, R. *Psychogenèse et histoire des sciences.* Paris: Flammarion, 1983. *Psychogenesis and the History of Science.* New York: Columbia University Press, 1989.

Reich, K. H. "Between Religion and Science: Complementarity in the Religious Thinking of Young People." *British Journal of Religious Education,* 1989a, *11,* 62–69.

Reich, K. H. *The Chalcedonian Definition: Which Logic?* Berichte zur Erziehungswissenschaft, nr. 78. Fribourg, Switzerland: Pädagogisches Institut der Universität Fribourg, 1989b.

Reich, K. H. "Commonalities and Differences of Piagetian Operations and Complementarity Reasoning: A Conceptual Model and Its Support by Empirical Data." Paper presented at the Twentieth Anniversary Symposium of the Jean Piaget Society, Philadelphia, May 31–June 2, 1990a.

Reich, K. H. "The Chalcedonian Definition, an Example of the Difficulties and the Usefulness of Thinking in Terms of Complementarity?" *Journal of Psychology and Theology,* 1990b, *18* (2), 148–157.

Reich, K. H. "The Relation Between Science and Theology: The Case for Complementarity Revisited." *Zygon: Journal of Religion & Science,* 1990c, *25* (4), 365–385.

Reich, K. H., and Oser, F. K. "Konkret-operatorisches, formal-operatorisches und komplementäres Denken, Begriffs- und Theorieentwicklung: Welche Beziehungen?" [Concrete operations, formal operations, complementarity reasoning, concept and theory development: Which relationships?] In F. K. Oser and K. H. Reich (eds.), *Bericht über die Arbeitsgruppe Entwicklung von Denkprozessen und Argumentationsfiguren auf der 9.* Tagung Entwicklungspsychologie, September 18–21, 1989, Munich. Fribourg, Switzerland: Pädagogisches Institut der Universität Fribourg, 1990.

Russell, R. J. "The Fruitfulness of Complementarity for Three Theological Problems." Unpublished manuscript, Center for Theology and the Natural Sciences, University of California, Berkeley, 1989.

Secretan, P. "Komplementarität zwischen Dialektik und Analektik, Hinweise zu einer noetischen Klärung des Komplementaritätsbegriffs" [Complementarity between dialectics and analectics. Toward a noetic clarification of the concept of complementarity]. In R. Oerter (ed.), *Bericht über das Symposium Jenseits des formal-logischen Denkens: Komplementäres und dialektisches Denken auf der 8.* Tagung Entwicklungspsychologie, September 13–16, 1987, Bern. Munich, Germany: Psychologisches Institut der Universität, 1987.

Vieth, R. F. *Holy Power, Human Pain.* Bloomington, Ind.: Meyer-Stone, 1988.

K. Helmut Reich is research associate at the Pedagogical Institute, University of Fribourg, Fribourg, Switzerland.

In adolescence, beliefs and doubts about God and the Church are often experienced in terms of fulfilled and unfulfilled expectations.

Adolescents' Justifications for Faith or Doubt in God: A Study of Fulfilled and Unfulfilled Expectations

Karl Ernst Nipkow, Friedrich Schweitzer

Our topic here is the issue of God as considered by adolescents. We explore the developmental trajectory that this issue takes from childhood into adolescence and within adolescence itself. Our approach could be called phenomenological since we begin by looking at phenomena and by trying to avoid general assumptions about adolescence or the religion of adolescence. Such an approach seems justified given the diversity of adolescents' views on religion, ranging from unexamined adherence to critical refusal, to highly emotional commitment, to open indifference.

Our starting point here is a collection of statements about God written by students between sixteen and twenty-two years of age. The results of our analysis are presented according to the content of the texts and to what the texts tell us about changes from childhood to adolescence. In a second step, we look at these results through the lenses of psychoanalytic and cognitive-developmental theories in order to determine how each perspective further illuminates our data. We chose these two theoretical approaches because they appear to offer the most coherent analyses of religion in adolescence. Also, they are sufficiently different from one another to offer a useful comparison.

Finally, for two reasons, we look closely at how adolescents talk about the relationship between God and the Church. First, the relationship between God and the Church is frequently addressed by adolescents. Second, discussion of this relationship has been absent in existing theories of religious development.

New Directions for Child Development, no. 52, Summer 1991 © Jossey-Bass Inc., Publishers

Changing Conceptions of God from Childhood into Adolescence

Sample and Procedure. Students (ages sixteen to twenty-two) in south-western Germany, from about seventy classrooms in vocational schools, were asked to write down their reflections and feelings about God. Almost all contributed to Schuster's (1984) collection of 1,236 statements, which were responses either to open-ended sentences (for example, "I believe/do not believe in God because . . . ") or to quotations (for example, "Beware of those people whose God is in the heavens"). The students' statements were subjected to inductive interpretation following a process akin to that described by Glaser and Strauss (1967): Categories describing students' responses were constructed on the basis of attentive listening and constant comparison rather than borrowed from existing theories.

Analysis of our students' statements revealed the following general result: Most students had challenging questions about God that frequently irritated them and moved them to seek answers. This result may not generalize to all adolescents, even in Germany, but it makes visible a number of crucial characteristics of religious development in adolescence. Students' statements indicated four distinct conceptions of God, each referring to a different *expectation*. Furthermore, whether or not expectations had been or were being fulfilled seemed to determine whether or not belief in God was sustained.

Expectations About God. The first expectation considered God as helper and as guarantor for the goodness of the world. For many of the students, the issue of God was almost exclusively related to experience of personal and pragmatic assistance in daily life, for example, "I do not believe in God. . . . In the past when I prayed to him because I was in a jam, he never helped me."

This first expectation was most apparent around the question of theodicy or why God allows evil and "innocent" suffering. The majority of our students did not relate this question to worldwide problems but rather to inexplicable suffering in their own neighborhoods or within their own groups of friends, for example, "I do not believe in God, for I had to see so many terrible things, good friends dying in accidents. . . . How can such things happen without God helping?"

The second expectation considered God as key to explaining the world. Here, the context was more cognitive than emotional or pragmatic. Questions concerned the origins of the universe as well as death and the meaning of death. Concerning the origins of the universe, the relationship between creation and evolution was frequently addressed, often through speculative ideas and questions, such as "If there is a God, how did he enter the void or the universe?" Concerning death, there was often anxiety and speculation, for example, "There must be something that goes on anyway, . . . perhaps with a new life or with eternal life." But the speculation did not involve reference to the Christian understanding of resurrection, which seemed to have little meaning for this group.

The third expectation considered the reality of God or whether God is more than just a word or symbol. This concern showed clearly in the following statement: "Whether God exists or not, I don't know. But I sometimes simply need an idea that helps me manage. Maybe God is only a sort of dreamed-of imagination or wish; this will always be an open question for me." There is ambiguity here, ambiguity stemming from how verification of God's existence depends on how God as dream, wish, or symbol functions for the individual. Feuerbach's (1957) critique of the idea of God as wishful thinking is always at hand and, in fact, was alluded to by many of the students in our sample.

The fourth and last expectation considered not God per se but rather the Church as God's witness. Here, the expectation was that the preaching of the Church makes sense and that the members of the Church act as models of goodness and spirituality. The students' statements indicate that they wondered if the Church is a trustworthy witness to God. They criticized adult church members for acting in ways contrary to true faith and for attending church out of social rather than religious motives. At the same time, they questioned what the Church teaches and did not find in the Church convincing answers to their questions about God.

Expectations and Development. Does the meaning of these four expectations derive in part from their place in the students' development? The students seem to say yes. They often spoke about their current ideas and questions, contrasting them with earlier thoughts from their childhood, for example, "Earlier, as a child, or rather until age thirteen, I believed in God just like children believe in God" and "I believed in God without asking or having doubts." The students perceived within themselves their movement from an unquestioning faith in childhood to a faith in adolescence based largely on questions.

From our perspective rather than from that of the students, the statements reveal a considerable range of ideas about God that fall at different levels or stages of religious development. The range is from simple and concrete ideas about God to very elaborate, abstract, and critically considered descriptions. Even among the oldest students there were those who imagined God as a "strong man with long white hair and a white beard." Others among this group imagined God as "an abstract principle of thought which is beyond the boundaries of imagination." Still others were within these two extremes, saying that they had images of God but the images were indefinite.

Of course, this was a cross-sectional study, which did not allow us to view development within given individuals. However, we assume that the statements reveal developmental shifts or absences of shifts; it seems to us unlikely that someone who considers God a "principle of thought" would move on to consider God as a "strong man with a white beard." We are supported in this assumption by a number of parallel studies (Babin, 1965; Vergote, 1970; Heller, 1986), each confirming that between childhood and adolescence there is a shift from a concrete and often-unquestioned image of God to a critical examination, and sometimes repudiation, of the image.

Interpretation of Statements Through the Lenses of Psychoanalytic and Cognitive-Developmental Theories

Here, we look at our data through the lenses of psychoanalytic and cognitive-developmental theories in order to see what light they can or cannot shed on our data.

Psychoanalytic Lens. Erikson (1958, 1968) understood adolescence as a process that takes its course between the polar opposites of identity and identity confusion (also see Wright, 1982). In this process, identity is achieved through selective integration of all childhood identifications, a process at once both painful and creative. Furthermore, this process of finding or constructing an identity is not solipsistic. Rather, it entails determining one's place in society and history, space and time.

Erikson observed that in determining their place in society adolescents often adopt or construct ideologies that support their sense of personal identity. These ideologies are marked by simplistic explanations and sharp divisions between friends and foes, good and evil, and so on, explanations and divisions that hold true neither for outward reality nor for the inner reality of feelings. For Erikson, the (over-) simplification of reality as pictured in adolescent ideologies functions to "screen" reality in much the same way that the mother serves to screen reality for the young child. And for Erikson (1968, p. 220) God functions not simply as a superego for the adolescent but also as the One who affirms a sense of being.

What does Erikson's perspective reveal about the statements of our students? First, we understand that the students' questions about God are not simply intellectual questions. Rather, they are existential questions that provide the meaning on which the adolescent's fragile identity rests. Second, we see in some students' statements (for example, "Whoever needs faith . . . belongs in a crazy house") the kind of ideological thinking presumed to function as a means to protect from reality and not simply to represent reality. We see that students' verbal statements may be far more clear-cut than their inner feelings and true convictions.

Also from a psychoanalytic point of view, Rizzuto (1979) traces the development of the "God representation" or intrapsychic images of God. According to Rizzuto, the God representation is constructed and reconstructed out of early and ongoing object relations so that the God representation, one's sense of self, and one's relation to reality are interdependent.

Belief in God, then, depends on a positive relationship between the God representation and the "object and self-representations needed to maintain a sense of self which provides at least a minimum of relatedness and hope" (Rizzuto, 1979, p. 202).

From this object relations perspective, we can see in our students a struggle with images and identifications stemming from childhood: "Only much later . . . I realized that I believed in God because my parents did as well." The adolescents' new sense of self, then, no longer can rest on identificatory participation in their parents' beliefs. Furthermore, their childhood images of God no longer fit their adolescent selves and, like the teddy bear of old, need to be put aside or only cherished in secret.

The psychoanalytic lens, therefore, offers us a clearer view by pointing beyond our students' statements to the unconscious images and tasks that influenced the construction of their statements. But this lens says little about cognitive structures that may explain both the advent of new statements about God and the differences between statements from one adolescent to the next. For this kind of analysis, we turn to cognitive-developmental theory.

Cognitive-Developmental Lens. In general, cognitive-developmental approaches to adolescence describe the adolescent as a "philosopher" whose discovery of the subjective self leads to a critical questioning of adult convictions and a (temporary) belief that everyone's perspective is equally correct and justified (Kohlberg and Gilligan, 1971; Perry, 1970). This picture of adolescent thinking seems applicable to our data. In our data, many of the students had moved away from what they considered to be childhood convictions to a state of questioning. Furthermore, the basis of their questioning was always to some degree their personal experience and their own ways of making sense of the world. At the same time, their challenges to conventional religious doctrine and adult religious convictions put them in a relativist position parallel to the relativism found in cognitive and moral domains.

In a similar but more specific vein, Fowler (1981) outlines a two-step move in adolescent religious thinking: a step from Mythic-Literal faith (holding an idiosyncratic faith but believing it to be the same as that held by adults) to Synthetic-Conventional faith (adopting the faith of one's group), and then a step to Individuative-Reflective faith (constructing autonomous faith not necessarily coordinated with that of the group). During this process, the adolescent takes on different perspectives with regard to religious symbols or images: from construing symbols as literally true (that is, viewing them not as symbols but as "facts") to interpreting them as symbols (usually with conventional meanings), to demythologizing them (that is, treating them as "mere" symbols and hence dispensable).

We see Fowler's distinctions, particularly his distinctions concerning the treatment of symbols, in our students' statements: from the Mythic-Literal statements about God being an old man or superman ("It seems to me that God is a higher being with a development beyond human possibilities"), to statements appreciating and valuing conventional religious symbols as symbols ("God is something like the air above us . . . the air which we need for life"), to statements serving to demythologize ("God, that's just a word, nothing else"). We do not see statements expressing the kind of reappreciation for symbols that comes with increased development.

Oser takes a slightly different focus when describing religious development in adolescence. Oser's focus is on the changing definitions of the God-person relationship and the influence that those definitions have on religious judgment (see Oser, this volume). According to Oser, individuals often enter adolescence with a *do et des* ('give so that you may receive') relationship with God in which God responds in kind to whatever individuals do or fail to do. From our data, a clear example of Stage 2 (*do et des*) thinking is the following statement: "If you make him angry, his temper gets awful, and he can punish you. But if you act the way he wants you to, he also rewards you."

Again, according to Oser, adolescents often become dissatisfied with this notion that we cut deals with God. Furthermore, they realize that life is not always "fair," that early death and serious illness come even to the innocent. Stage 2 thinking is replaced by a new emphasis on human autonomy, responsibility, and independence, often at the expense of God's autonomy and influence. From our data, the following is an example: "We must help ourselves; God can only be a comfort, a support for us and no magician."

Most often, however, the adolescents in our sample seemed to be caught between Stages 2 and 3. They rejected Stage 2 thinking, but without having achieved a different, workable conception. They were fixated on the problem of evil and suffering—the problem of theodicy—which they saw simply in terms of failed reciprocity between God and humans.

With respect to the problem of theodicy, many of the adolescents thought of God as ultimately responsible for what happens in the world and questioned why God is "so cruel to human beings." There was an emerging notion of an overall "plan" of God (Stage 4 in Oser's scheme), but this notion was not elaborated, for example, "I also believe that when you pray God hears your prayer, even if it is not fulfilled there is certainly a reason for this." It is noteworthy that although the students were brought up in the Christian tradition, their statements generally did not reflect a view of God as compassionate.

Reich (this volume, 1989) has described five levels of complementarity reasoning, that is, reasoning used to render seemingly incompatible explanations noncompatible (neither compatible nor incompatible). Examples of only the first three levels can be found in our data, all of which deal with the issue of whether the origins of the world are best accounted for by the biblical creation story or by the scientific theory of evolution. Most of the statements concerning creation and evolution raised questions based on simple either-or alternatives (Level 1), some accepted the possibility that both views may be right (Level 2), and only very few assumed that both are in fact needed (Level 3). In other words, development of complementarity reasoning was, at best, incipient with these adolescents.

Reich observes that in childhood both views (creation and evolution) are accepted and that in adolescence this acceptance becomes a conscious coordination and reasoned affirmation. However, such coordination and affirmation are rare in our data. In most cases we find instead a critical examination and rejection of one side (usually the creation or religious side). As Reich suggests, this rejection may be due to secular influences in the culture, or it might be a transitional phenomenon that will give way to mature complementarity reasoning. Our data do not allow for a definitive answer.

Two Questions. In concluding this discussion of the value of psychoanalytic and cognitive-developmental theories, two questions need to be addressed. First, what do the theories account for in the adolescents' conceptions of God and what do they leave out? Second, how are we to define the relationship between these two theories of religious development?

Concerning the first question, the theories have helped us interpret our material. Since our data were collected independently of the theories, their utility in interpretation suggests their meaningfulness and an interpretive power extending beyond the data from which they originally were derived. However, the theories did not help us interpret statements concerning the fourth expectation, the Church as God's witness. Our data indicate that this fourth expectation played a major part in the adolescents' thinking about God and religion, hence we discuss this expectation in greater depth in the next section.

Concerning the second question, it is clear that the psychoanalytic and cognitive-developmental theories work with different foci. However, their relationship is complementary rather than competitive.

God and the Church: A Neglected Connection

When the adolescents in our sample thought about God, they often thought about the Church. Furthermore, their perception of the Church influenced their understanding of God, and usually this influence was negative. Statements such as the following were typical: "People are eager to go to church only so they will go to heaven or because God allegedly doesn't like it when one does not pray or go to church." "People attend church because they want to look like Christians, but they really are hypocrites." "Religion has become too much of a business in which sometimes considerable profits can be made."

For the many adolescents who criticized the Church there was a solution, namely, differentiating between *the religion of the Church* and *their own religion as individuals.* They challenged the assumption that to be religious is equivalent to being in, or in agreement with, the Church: "The Church is not needed because *if* you believe in something, you can believe it at home as well." "The attitude of the Church . . . has long been dated but religion is really modern."

A minority of the students provided a positive picture of the Church. These few considered the Church a place of silence, a place where God's closeness can be experienced. Or they saw it as a community that gives "the feeling that he (God) must exist."

If we assume that affirmation of individual faith over faith of the Church presupposes a critical perspective on the Church as an institution, we conclude that there are three developmental levels operative in our data: The first is an unquestioning acceptance of the Church as a place of worship, the second is a critical questioning of the Church as an institution, and the third is the affirmation of individual faith over faith of the Church. As is often the case with other religious issues, complex and differentiated understandings of the Church, as taught by Christian theology, were not evidenced in our students' statements, for example, distinctions between the local church and worldwide Church, between the visible church and invisible Church, and between the Church as part of this world versus another.

Our data do not suggest a developmental model for understanding conceptions of the Church. However, the data and our subsequent reflection on them suggest that the following model might prove useful in the future:

The Church as a Building (a House That Is God's Dwelling Place). This conception can be found in childhood but rarely in adolescence.

The Church as a Local Group of Worshippers. The extension here is to the people, services, and activities taking place within a building.

The Church as an Institution That Is Critically Considered. Here the Church is seen as a social organization with purposes, forms, means, and doctrines. At this level, reforming the Church means changing purposes or beliefs.

Distinction Between Personal and Institutional Religion. Again, the Church is seen as an institution that has to be criticized for its failure to live up to religious standards, but one's own faith is now claimed as "true religion." This religious self-affirmation of the individual appears as a major step in adolescence. Often the possibility of maintaining belief in God rests on this possibility of affirming a personal faith that does not fit the faith of any church. The realization that one can be religious and yet not go along with a particular church is not found before adolescence.

The Local and Worldwide, Visible and Invisible, This-Worldly and Other-Worldly, Real and Ideal Church. As we can only draw upon theological definitions here, this description is simply a preliminary suggestion for an end point. It is a suggestion that individuals can appreciate the Church *after* critical distinctions are made between the real and ideal, the personal and the institutional.

Conclusion

In this chapter, we have limited our analysis to psychological theories of religious development. But can psychology offer a sufficient explanation of the changes that it describes? It seems that the answer is no. We need to consider additional approaches that look at society and culture, as well as at the role that religion plays in them.

There is, then, another task still to be done once psychological explanations have been given. We need to interpret religious development in its social and cultural contexts. Our guiding hypothesis is that these contexts can be characterized as "post-Christian," by which we mean that there is a strong current of Christian tradition, but at the same time there are conditions that continually alter and disperse that current.

References

Babin, P. "The Idea of God: Its Evolution Between the Ages of 11 and 19." In A. Godin (ed.), *From Religious Experience to a Religious Attitude*. Chicago: Loyola University Press, 1965.

Erikson, E. H. *Young Man Luther: A Study in Psychoanalysis and History*. New York: Norton, 1958.

Erikson, E. H. *Identity, Youth, and Crisis*. New York: Norton, 1968.

Feuerbach, L. *The Essence of Christianity*. New York: Harper & Row, 1957.

Fowler, J. W. *Stages of Faith: The Psychology of Human Development and the Quest for Meaning*. New York: Harper & Row, 1981.

Glaser, B. G., and Strauss, A. L. *A Discovery of Grounded Theory: Strategies for Qualitative Research*. New York: Aldine, 1967.

Heller, D. *The Children's God*. Chicago: University of Chicago Press, 1986.

Kohlberg, L., and Gilligan, C. "The Adolescent as a Philosopher: The Discovery of the Self in a Postconventional World." *Daedalus*, 1971, *100*, 1051–1086.

Perry, W. G., Jr. *Forms of Intellectual and Ethical Development in the College Years: A Scheme*. New York: Holt, Rinehart & Winston, 1970.

Reich, K. H. "Between Religion and Science: Complementarity in the Religious Thinking of Young People." *British Journal of Religious Education*, 1989, *11* (2), 62–69.

Rizzuto, A.-M. *The Birth of the Living God: A Psychoanalytic Study*. Chicago: University of Chicago Press, 1979.

Schuster, R. (ed.). *Was sie glauben: Texte von Jugendlichen* [What they believe: texts by adolescents]. Stuttgart, Germany: Steinkopf, 1984.

Vergote, A. *Religionspsychologie* [Psychology of religion]. Olten and Freiburg, Germany: Walter, 1970.

Wright, J. E., Jr. *Erikson: Identity and Religion*. New York: Seabury, 1982.

Karl Ernst Nipkow is professor of religious education and general education, University of Tübingen, Tübingen, Germany.

Friedrich Schweitzer is lecturer in religious education, University of Tübingen, Tübingen, Germany.

Biblical parables are interpreted through the lens of one's stage of religious judgment, as described by Oser and Gmünder.

Understanding Parables: A Developmental Analysis

Anton A. Bucher

Theory and Purpose

In the early 1960s, Ronald Goldman (1964) provided an insightful analysis of children's understanding of parables. That analysis explained the development of religious thinking from a Piagetian perspective. Development of thinking about parables, then, was explained in terms of Piaget's stages of intuitive (pre-operational), concrete-operational, and formal operational thinking. Although the Goldman study marked a significant step beyond mere description of changes with age, it did not give us a way to understand the development of religious thinking as a unique domain calling for unique structures of thought. The study here assumed that religious thinking is derived from both general Piagetian and specific religious thought structures.

Those specific religious thought structures have been defined in the research of Oser and Gmünder (1988; see Oser, this volume). Though their work is reviewed elsewhere in this volume, it is useful here to summarize essentials. In brief, religious judgment (thinking) depends on how we structure the God-person relationship. Furthermore, understanding of this relationship develops as a progression of stages described as follows: In Stage 1, the Ultimate Being protects or hurts, dispenses health or illness, and influences each of us directly but without our influence and control (deus ex machina). The Ultimate Being is an anthropomorphic and powerful being who intervenes directly into the affairs of people. In Stage 2, the Ultimate Being continues to be humanlike and to act directly, but now he or she can be influenced by prayers, offerings, adherence to religious rules, and so on (*do et des*, 'give so that you may receive'). In Stage 3, we assume full responsibility for our lives; transcendence is outside ourselves and may be either rejected or doubted as irrelevant to everyday living. In Stage 4, the Ultimate Being becomes the condition for human freedom, independence, and so on via the divine plan. And in Stage Five, the Ultimate Being inhabits each human interactional commitment but also transcends it at the same time. The purpose of my pilot study was to show just how the Oser-Gmünder model helps explain the development of understanding of parables.

The Study

Twenty-eight Swiss subjects, ages seven to fifty (equally divided between male and female and half younger than thirteen), were tested for their respective stages of religious judgment using Oser and Gmünder's "Paul dilemma." This vignette asks subjects to judge whether someone who had just survived an airplane crash should carry out a promise made to God as the plane was about to crash (see Oser, this volume). In addition, subjects were engaged in semistructured interviews about their understanding of two parables from the New Testament: the parable of the laborers in the vineyard (Matt. 20:1–16) and the parable of the talents (Matt. 25:14–30). The first parable tells a story of a master who hires laborers, for all or part of one day, to work his vineyard and pays them all the same regardless of the time of day they were hired. In this parable, the laborers hired at the beginning of the day object to the equal pay being given to those hired later. The second parable tells a story of a master who entrusts his property or "talents" to three servants while he goes on a journey. Upon his return, the master rewards the two servants who had invested his property wisely and punishes the servant who had simply buried it in the ground for safekeeping.

   Levels of Understanding. The protocols and results revealed three levels of how parables are understood.

   Level 1: Concrete-Literal. The youngest children took the parables to be true stories about events in Jesus's time. Here is an example from a seven-year-old:

INTERVIEWER: Do you think this story (parable of the laborers in the vineyard) really happened?
CHILD: Sure.
INTERVIEWER: And where did it happen?
CHILD: Abroad, somewhere, when Jesus was alive.
INTERVIEWER: And in our village might a story that means the same happen here also?
CHILD: No, it won't.

INTERVIEWER: And why?
CHILD: Because Jesus wasn't here; he couldn't have seen it.

When pressed as to possible religious analogies in the parables—for example, "Might the master in the story be an image of God himself?"—the youngest children gave responses such as the following: "No, because God is in the sky, and the master is in the vineyard." "The master doesn't look like God." "God has a long white coat, but the master, he has pants." "If he [the master] had a beard, he would be an image of God. But the beard must be white and very long up to the belly."

Level 2: Concrete-Moral. Individuals at this level understood the parables as fiction with a message. However, the message was about simple, moral "truths" such as "people have to work," rather than about theological concepts such as the kingdom of God. Furthermore, the subjects showed a beginning capacity to draw analogies between the parables and their own understanding and use of religious terms. For example, one ten-year-old said that the master of the vineyard is an image of God "because we say God is the master too."

Level 3: Symbolic-Analogical. Only persons at this level fully appreciated the function of parables. Spontaneously, they treated the stories as fiction, containing a deep meaning about religious concepts that could not be said as effectively in another way. Furthermore, persons at this level saw many, often complex analogies that mapped characters and events to religious beliefs. For example, one individual saw the parable of the talents as meaning the following: "By the talents, I think that means really the love. God gives it to us, and we have to augment it."

Two judges scored the protocols using a description system that elaborates on the three levels (Bucher, 1990). The coefficient of interrater reliability was .89. Results of statistical analyses supported the expected age trend as well as the expected correspondence between Oser and Gmünder's stages of religious judgment and the levels of understanding outlined above.

Interpretations and Religious Judgment. The results so far stay close to Goldman's findings. However, the protocols provided much more to analyze. Specifically, the protocols revealed a number of different ways in which the parables were interpreted. The question was whether these interpretations reflected individuals' stages of religious judgment (thinking) as measured by Oser and Gmünder's (1988) scheme. It was assumed that stage of religious judgment, not age, would be the primary determinant of how parables were interpreted, as evidenced by an isomorphism between the form of thinking characteristic of a given stage and the form of thinking in a given interpretation. (None of the subjects in the sample functioned at Stage 5, so in the following discussion I report findings for Stages 1-4 only.)

Those scoring at about Stage 1 for religious judgment interpreted the laborers parable as a warning that we should not be envious and should not complain. Most of this group was made up of the younger children. But one twenty-five-year-old woman at Stage 1 responded to the question of what the story meant as follows: "That we shouldn't be envious because the master will be angry, likewise God, he will punish us [if we are envious]." Here, then, the parable has been assimilated to her Stage 1 understanding of the God-person relationship. The master and God are both seen as powerful, even vengeful, authorities demanding obedience and good behavior.

Subjects at about Stage 2 did not view the laborers parable as reflecting anything about the true nature of God. For example, an eleven-year-old girl, when asked whether and why the master of the vineyard could be an image of God, answered, "That's impossible because God is just. If someone works the whole day, he [God] gives fifty francs. If someone works only one hour, he gives much less; he gives exactly five francs." The interviewer then confronted her with a common theological interpretation by saying, "But there are some people who say that God is kind, that he gives more than he needs to give, that he acts just like the master. What do you think?" She replied, "That's wrong, because God is just." The emphasis here, then, is on the humanlike and reciprocal nature of the God-person relationship, as expected from Stage 2 thinking.

In Stage 3, the focus shifts from God to persons; the emphasis is on individual responsibility, on the belief that fate is in our hands. Subjects at this stage reflected this emphasis in their interpretation of the laborers parable. These subjects saw the act of becoming a laborer as analogous to joining the Church. The parable's meaning to them lay in the observation that it is never too late for us to change, or as one subject said when asked about the parable's meaning, "that we can change our life, whenever we like. It is of no consequence whether it be the morning, that is, in our youth, or the evening, that is, in our old age. The most important thing is that one really wants to change."

In Stage 4, the focus is again on God and his nature, will, and actions, but without the anthropomorphisms of the first two stages. Stage 4 subjects interpreted the parable as analogous to God's kindness, which does not follow usual standards for when and how to be kind. These subjects saw in the parable the message that God wants the best for people, especially the poor and sinful. The rich wage given to the latecomers was appreciated as a convincing image of God's grace. For example, one fifty-year-old woman saw in the master's repeated search for new laborers an image of God's persistence and effort to help. Furthermore, she remembered that in her childhood she had considered the master unjust, and later as quite different from God. Only after becoming a mother did she begin to interpret the parable in the way she reported to the interviewer. She thus gave vivid proof of the supposition that listeners or readers of parables interpret meaning through the filter of their respective stages of religious judgment.

Similar results were found when analyzing interpretations of the parable of the talents. The following types of interpretations corresponded with the expected levels of religious judgment:

Type 1: The parable warns against punishment.

Type 2: The parable teaches that God rewards the industrious and punishes the lazy.

Type 3: The parable invites the listener/reader to be responsible and active and to avoid bringing trouble upon oneself, as happened with the third servant.

Type 4: The parable is rejected out of the belief that God does not reward and punish like the master.

Conclusion

This pilot study, then, provides empirical evidence that biblical parables are interpreted through the lens of one's stage of religious judgment, as described by Oser and Gmünder. Obviously, this conclusion does not contradict the findings of Goldman. Rather, it supplements the Piagetian explanations by providing a closer look at how interpretations are fashioned.

Two final points are worth mentioning. First, we can assume that what is said here about parables applies to the development of understanding and interpretation of Scripture in general. It would be odd, indeed, if we used our stage of religious judgment to interpret parables but then used different thought structures to interpret psalms, homilies, and so on.

Second, the evidence here supports an old, but often-forgotten idea that theology or the wisdom of mature religious thinking cannot be passed on directly to new generations. Wisdom, whether or not "religious," comes after years of active interpretation and reinterpretation. Religious educators, then, need to be patient, empathic, and tolerant when confronted with the immature theology of the young.

References

Bucher, A. A. Gleichnisverständnisse verstehen lernen. Strukturgenetische Untersuchungen zur Rezeption synoptischer Parabeln [Learning to understand parables: Structural research on reception of synoptic parables]. Fribourg: Universitätsverlag, 1990.

Goldman, R. Religious Thinking from Childhood to Adolescence. New York: Seabury, 1964.

Oser, F. K., and Gmünder, P. (eds.). Der Mensch—Stufen seiner religiösen Entwicklung [Stages of human religious development: A developmental approach]. Gütersloh, Germany: Gerd Mohn, 1988.

Anton A. Bucher is assistant professor at the Pedagogical Institute, University of Fribourg, Fribourg, Switzerland.

Brief comments on references (roughly of the last decade) considered helpful for further study are presented, excluding those listed in the various chapters of this volume. Areas covered are religion and psychology, measurement of religiousness, religious development over the life cycle, religious experience, conversion, religion and morality, and images of God.

Annotated Bibliography on Religious Development

Anton A. Bucher, K. Helmut Reich

The history of the psychology of religion in the United States is one marked by ups and downs rather than by continuous progress. By the early nineteenth century American psychology was already exhibiting one of the problems that would beset it later on as well, namely, the nature of the relationship between psychology and theology. While some researchers shunned theology, a position typified by Asa Mahan's 1845 claim that "we must confine ourselves strictly and exclusively to the laws of psychological investigation, without reference to any system of theology" (Spilka, 1987, p. 5), others (for example, James McCosh and Noah Porter; see Spilka, 1987) mixed psychology and theology in a way hardly conducive to establishing the psychology of religion as a scientific discipline. Nevertheless, at the time this did not stop the founding parents of American psychology from taking a deep interest in religion. William James, G. Stanley Hall, Edwin Starbuck, and James Leuba all made substantial contributions to the field (Gorsuch, 1988).

In contrast, from 1930 to 1960, the psychology of religion was almost extinct. Gorsuch (1988, pp. 203-205) proposes several hypotheses to explain this development, such as the "need" of professional psychologists to distance themselves from philosophy and the related discipline of theology while they established psychology as an autonomous scientific discipline. Also, what little activity there was during this time did not encourage others to take the psychology of religion seriously. Vande Kemp (1986, pp. 101-105) draws attention to the tug-of-war between the pro- and anti-religionist psychologists of religion, both groups being apt to commit the error of unwarranted movement from psychology to ontology in their zeal to prove the basic theses of their respective positions.

The rebirth of interest in the psychology of religion after 1960 was due to a new orientation of psychology—a turn away from behaviorism and toward cognition and even moral psychology—as well as to a renewed interest by theologians in psychology (Gorsuch, 1988, pp. 2-3). Also, having learned from the difficulties of the past, practitioners of the new psychology of religion expressly abstained from making any assumptions or denials regarding the truth of religion that is perceived by believers as directly revealed by God. The new psychology confined itself to understanding. Thus, Paul Pruyser (Vande Kemp, 1986, p. 3) asserted, "It is a perfectly psychological question to ask why and on what grounds some people answer the ontological question about their god vigorously in the affirmative, why some deny it, and why a third group say that they do not know. . . . The ontological question with capital letters is one thing, but every individual's way of coming to grips with it is quite a different thing."

With this brief historical sketch as a context, apart from a few classics the following, annotated bibliography reviews some recent references (roughly of the last decade) considered helpful for further study, excluding those listed in the various chapters of this volume.

Religion and Psychology

Barnes, M., Kahoe, R. D., and Kwilecki, S. "Debate on the Goals of Religious Development According to Particular Traditions and to Scientific Theories." *Religion,* 1988, *18,* 231-251; *Journal for the Scientific Study of Religion,* 1988, *27,* 307-325; *Journal for the Scientific Study of Religion,* 1989, *28,* 230-232, 233-236, 237-240.

These five single-author articles bring out commonalities and differences between the two types of goals (see Meadow and Kahoe, 1984) and demonstrate the difficulty of a synoptic view or even of dialogue.

Bergin, A. E., Ellis, A., and Walls, G. B. "A Debate on Theistic Religious and Atheistic Humanistic Values." *Journal of Consulting and Clinical Psychology,* 1980, *48,* 95-105, 635-639, 640-641, 642-645; *Professional Psychology,* 1983, *14,* 170-184.

The issue at stake in these five articles is the extent to which religion should be taken into account in theories, research, and techniques bearing on personality and psychotherapy. The debate also shows the difficulty of a knowledgeable, unbiased dialogue between representatives of worldviews that differ so fundamentally.

Gartner, J. "Religious Prejudice in Psychology: Theories of Its Cause and Cure." *Journal of Psychology and Christianity,* 1985, *4* (1), 16-23.

After listing instances of religious prejudice (negative descriptions of religious people, bias of personality tests against religious people, neglect of religious experience and behavior in psychology texts, and so on), the author analyzes conceivable explanations from a psychodynamic, sociocultural, and cognitive perspectives and indicates possible cures.

Godin, A. *The Psychological Dynamics of Religious Experience.* Birmingham, Ala.: Religious Education Press, 1985.

Godin explains which aspects of the Christian faith do not serve religious functions, as sometimes conceived (projection or wish fulfillment). He uses psychological criteria to examine how Christian experience could be other than an illusion and what that means for religious development.

Gorsuch, R. L. "Psychology of Religion." *Annual Review of Psychology,* 1988, *39,* 201–221.

Gorsuch describes briefly the history of the psychology of religion and sketches several theories about the decline and rebirth of that branch of psychology that involve both psychologists and theologians. He discusses also research on religion within other areas of psychology.

Hunter, W. F. (ed.). *The Case for Theological Literacy in the Psychology of Religion.* Special issue of *Journal of Psychology & Theology,* 1990, *17* (4), 327–393.

The contributors (W. F. Hunter, M. J. Donahue, R. W. Hood, Jr., B. Spilka and R. A. Bridges, R. N. Williams, C. B Taylor and W. J. Hintze, B. R. Hertel, R. S. Anderson, R. F. Paloutzian, and W. M. Goldsmith), all psychologists of religion, consider the dangers and possible benefits of increased interaction between psychology and theology. One gets a sense that knowledge of theology can make for more sophisticated research in the psychology of religion.

Lee, C. "The Dialogue of Theology with Experimental Psychology: A Historical Prolegomenon." *Studia Biblica et Theologica,* 1986, *14* (2), 145–174.

Lee limits his review to experimental psychology, as opposed to psychoanalysis, Gestalt theory, and so on. He aims at a "cooperative partnership" between the two fields of theology and psychology. In formulating a solid foundation for this partnership, Lee reviews the development of psychology from Hume and Locke to Kant, Herbart, Fechner, Wundt, and his American students (Cattell, Hall, and Tichener). However, according to Lee, whereas American psychologists of that period got their practices from Wundt, their principles came from Charles Darwin (compare Spilka, 1987). After consideration of William James, John Dewey, and John D. Watson, Lee concludes that psychology—which has continuously moved along in step with the (changing) philosophy of science—is getting ready for a deeper discussion with theology, including the metaphysical assumptions and underpinnings of each approach. Lee envisages that communication between the mutually skeptical fields of theology and psychology will be facilitated by those who are academically bilingual.

Meadow, M. J., and Kahoe, R. D. "Psychological Versus Spiritual Maturity." In M. J. Meadow and R. D. Kahoe, *Psychology of Religion: Religion in Individual Lives.* New York: Harper & Row, 1984.

Arguing from a psychological perspective, these authors differentiate among mature religious *visions* (comprehensive, unifying philosophy of life, critical evaluation of faith, heuristic nature of mature belief, unitive consciousness), mature religious *striving* (extension of ego boundaries, autonomous and effective motivation, living with insecurity, altruistic services to others), and mature religious *attitudes* (self-objectivity, acceptance of human foibles, mature conscience and values, avoidance of idolatries). Spiritual maturity may involve goals different from those advocated by psychology, for instance, renunciation (in Hinduism) or facing up to ever-stronger spiritual tribulations (Martin Luther). Whereas some goals may be common to the two disciplines (maintaining dialogue and self-disclosure, going beyond conscious awareness, continuing self-observation and evaluation of life events, refining one's theoretical framework for making value judgments, and so on), the differences indicated lead the authors to conclude that "religion and psychology cannot replace each other, though they may enrich each other" (p. 399).

Spilka, B. "Religion and Science in Early American Psychology." *Journal of Psychology and Theology,* 1987, *15,* 3–9.

Spilka argues that, contrary to the present mutual skepticism of theology and psychology, religion was an active and often constructive force in early American psychology (from 1800). This enrichment of psychology was largely due to the common sense realism adopted by the Scottish philosophers-clerics who regarded nature as "one volume of God's Bible." Spilka also finds traces of those philosophical beginnings in the works of Baldwin and Dewey.

Spilka, B. "Psychology's Forgotten Religious Heritage." *Connecticut Review,* 1989, *11* (2), 78–89.

This article further develops the findings in Spilka (1987).

Timpe, R. L. "Epistemological and Metaphysical Limits to the Integration of Psychology and Theology." *Journal of Psychology and Christianity,* 1983, 2 (3), 21–29.

Timpe reviews four models of the relationship between psychology and theology: *versus* (only one of the disciplines possesses "truth"), *of* (one discipline is a subset of the other), *parallel* (although with some overlap), and *integrated*. The article deals mainly with the parallel relationship, defining the overlap area as one in which "the individual's behavior is a parcel of the ultimate concern" (pp. 23-24). This is the area of "providential" explanations. However, because of their diverse nature and content, psychology and religion should be kept separate but be considered equal.

Vande Kemp, H. "Dangers of Psychologism: The Place of God in Psychology." *Journal of Psychology and Theology*, 1986, *14* (2), 97-109.

This is another historical review, in which the meaning of psychology and of psychologism are explored in a very scholarly way. In her conclusions, the author cautions against an improper demarcation of the psychology of religion. For example, one cannot attempt to decrease the immensity of the religious leap of faith by means of psychological explanations.

Wulff, D. M. *Psychology of Religion: A Study of Classic and Contemporary Views.* New York: Wiley, 1991.

Wulff locates various approaches to the psychology of religion on a spectrum extending from the exclusion of transcendence (theoretical behaviorism, orthodox psychoanalysis) to the inclusion of the transcendent (study of Conjunctive faith). He argues that the actual experience of a perceived spiritual reality is a legitimate theme of psychological research (pp. 630-636).

Measurement of Religiousness

Brown, L. B. "The Measurement of Religion." In L. B. Brown, *The Psychology of Religious Belief.* London: Academic Press, 1987.

Brown, L. B. "Religious Measures." In L. B. Brown, *The Psychology of Religion: An Introduction.* London: SPCK, 1988.

Drawing from his long-standing experience, Brown, in these two citations, discusses the issues at hand in detail and draws attention to the pitfalls in which the unwary might fall, particularly with respect to the construction of questionnaires.

Burgard, P. "Zum Problem des Messens religioser Urteilstrukturen" [On the problem of measuring the stages of religious judgment]. In A. A. Bucher and K. H. Reich (eds.), *Entwicklung von Religiosität. Grundlagen—Theorieprobleme—Praktische Anwendung.* Fribourg, Switzerland: Universitätsverlag, 1989.

In this contribution the author outlines the specific problems of the measurement of religious judgment as conceptualized by Oser and Gmünder (see Oser, this volume).

Meadow, M. J., and Kahoe, R. D. "Dimensions of Religiousness." In M. J. Meadow and R. D. Kahoe, *Psychology of Religion: Religion in Individual Lives.* New York: Harper & Row, 1984.

The authors discuss different measurement approaches (unidimensional, bipolar dimensional, and so on), advocating in particular the application of multidimensional models.

Shaver, P. R. "Religious Attitudes." In J. P. Robinson and P. R. Shaver, *Measures of Social Psychological Attitudes.* (6th reprint) Ann Arbor: Survey Research Center, Institute for Social Research, University of Michigan, 1978.

This contribution contains seventeen scales on religion (for example, attitudes toward the Church and toward religious ideologies) as well as personal religiousness and belief. This work is very useful because it includes the items of the questionnaires as well as the necessary statistical instructions. But most of these scales refer to traditional religions and cannot be applied to new religious phenomena such as modern astrology, New Age, reincarnation, and spiritism.

Silverman, W. "Bibliography of Measurement Techniques Used in the Social Scientific Study of Religion." *Psychological Documents,* 1983, *13* (1).

The article contains bibliographical information on the topic of measurement techniques.

Spilka, B., Hood, R. W., Jr., and Gorsuch, R. L. "The Operational Definition of Religion." In B. Spilka, R. W. Hood, Jr., and R. L. Gorsuch, *The Psychology of Religion: An Empirical Approach.* Englewood Cliffs, N.J.: Prentice-Hall, 1985.

The best operational definition of religion is discussed in connection with problems of and different approaches to measuring religiousness. The authors outline religious typologies, trait approaches, and multitrait systems, which are needed because religion is a very complex phenomenon. Additionally, the authors provide a "technical appendix," that is, a brief instruction on the most important statistical terms and a review of empirical proceedings that are recommended especially for scientists of religion and theologians interested in conducting their own empirical research.

Religious Development over the Life Cycle

The publication of English-language books on the psychology of religion has clearly increased during the past decade. However, cognitive-developmental psychology is singularly missing in this context. In discussing the symposium that was the basis for his book *Advances in the Psychology of Religion* (Oxford, England: Pergamon Press, 1985), L. B. Brown writes, "That it proved impossible to find someone to read us a paper on religious development could indicate an unfortunate decline of interest in that field" (p. 4). For his short article on the psychology of religion, Gorsuch (1988) compresses projection, socialization, and cognitive-developmental theories into only one page devoted to religious development. None of the twelve chapters in Wulff's (1991) otherwise standard-setting volume on the psychology of religion deals specifically with cognitive-developmental theories (although Fowler's work is discussed in connection with that of Erik Erikson). Because of the scarcity of material on the complete life cycle, we also include references that cover only part of that cycle.

Broughton, J. M., and Freeman-Moir, J. (eds.). *The Developmental Psychology of J. M. Baldwin.* Norwood, N.J.: Ablex, 1982.

The recent rediscovery of the early twentieth-century work of James Mark Baldwin warrants attention, for Baldwin's efforts in the field of religious development are still valuable. He described four stages of religious development, emphasizing social as well as individual factors (including a "logic of emotion and interest"). In his discussion of the developmental mechanism, he introduced the dialectics of assimilation and accommodation, later popularized by Jean Piaget. Wallwork's contribution to this volume, an article titled "Religious Development," is noteworthy for the scholarly analysis of Baldwin's work.

Byrnes, J. F. *The Psychology of Religion.* New York: Free Press, 1984.

This textbook should help beginners orient themselves in the area of religious studies and psychological analysis. For instance, Byrnes attempts to "explain" as far as possible, the religious development of Augustinus, bishop of Hippo, by means of various psychological theories. In the body of the book there are expositions of the theories of James, Freud, Jung, Allport, Maslow, May, Erikson, and Piaget. The chapter on the influence of society on religious development deals with the theories of Festinger, Kelly, Fiske, Maddi, Mead, Goffman, Heilman, and Galanter.

Coles, R. *The Spiritual Life of Children.* Boston: Houghton Mifflin, 1990.

Written in a compelling narrative style and following in the tradition of Rizzuto (this volume), Coles provides a sympathetic picture of children as theologians struggling with the great issues of life.

Crapps, R. W. "Religion and Human Development: An Overview" and "The Development of Religious Thinking." In R. W. Crapps, *An Introduction to Psychology of Religion.* Macon, Ga.: Mercer University Press, 1986.

Crapps explains in simple language what human development in general and religious development in particular are about and refers to the works of Gleason, Piaget, Elkind, Spilka, Lang, Harms, Goldman, Erikson, Maves, Fowler, Pruyser, Allport, Festinger, Tillich, and Gilkey. The aim throughout is to present and discuss "data derived from serious inquiry into exchanges between psychology and religion since the turn of the twentieth century" (p. ix).

Meadow, M. J., and Kahoe, R. D. "Development of Religiousness in Individuals," "Stage Models of Development," and "Research in the Development of Religiousness." In M. J. Meadow and R. D. Kahoe, *Psychology of Religion: Religion in Individual Lives.* New York: Harper & Row, 1984.

The authors cover ground similar to that covered in Crapps (1986), but in a more technical language and with the provision of more research data. They also present their own model of religious development, which is an extension of the work by Batson, Broen, Brown, and Spilka: The developmental sequence goes from extrinsic religiosity to observance, to intrinsic religiosity, and (possibly) to autonomy.

Paloutzian, R. F. "Psychology of Religious Development." In R. F. Paloutzian, *Invitation to the Psychology of Religion.* Glenview, Ill.: Scott, Foresman, 1983.

Paloutzian provides a general background for the understanding of religious development and presents the findings of Piaget, Harms, Goldman, Elkind, Long, and Spilka. He also discusses religious development in adolescence and the factors involved. (This book also contains a well-documented chapter on the history of the psychology of religion in the United States, including a discussion of the factors involved in its decline and rebirth.)

Reich, K. H. "Religious Development Across the Life Span." In D. L. Featherman, R. M. Lerner, and M. Perlmutter (eds.), *Life-Span Development and Behavior: Conventional and Cognitive Developmental Approaches.* Vol. 12. Hillsdale, N.J.: Erlbaum, in press.

Reich presents data on religious development across the life span, including striking changes in faith, and discusses development and change in the light of the theories of Baldwin, Elkind, Erikson, Fowler, Goldman, Hall, Kahoe and Meadow, Oser and Gmünder, Rizzuto, Spranger, and others. He specifies the targets to be met by a pertinent overarching theory and suggests a way to approach its realization.

Slee, N. "Goldman yet Again, an Overview and Critique of His Contribution to Research." *British Journal of Religious Education,* 1986, 8, 84–93.

Goldman was the first to systematically apply Piaget's stage theory of intellectual development to religious thinking, and to explore empirically the resulting concepts. While pointing out certain weaknesses, Slee discusses the impact of Goldman's work on research, which was essentially the initiation of a fresh start to the study of religious development. Goldman also influenced religious education, including a revision of teaching material.

Spilka, B., Hood, R. W., Jr., and Gorsuch, R. L. "Childhood: Stages in Religious Development," "Impact of Family and Schools on Religious Development," and "Religion in Adult Life." In B. Spilka, R. W. Hood, Jr., and R. L. Gorsuch, *The Psychology of Religion: An Empirical Approach.* Englewood Cliffs, N.J.: Prentice-Hall, 1985.

The two chapters on childhood stages and adult religion correspond roughly in content to what is discussed by Byrnes (1984), Crapps (1986), and Meadow and Kahoe (1984), but more data are provided. The chapter on family and schools provides amplified insights into the impact of various external "offers." Overall, the presentation clearly concerns *elements* of an encompassing, consistent theory of religious development rather than such a theory as a whole.

Wulff, D. M. *Psychology of Religion: A Study of Classic and Contemporary Views.* New York: Wiley, 1991.

This is a thorough and up-to-date presentation of the subject, except for cognitive-developmental theories. It features a balanced assessment of the various approaches and sixty-eight pages of reference.

Religious Experience

Girgensohn, K. *Der seelische Aufbau des religiosen Erlebens. Eine religionspsychologischer Untersuchung auf experimenteller Grundlage* [The psychic structure of religious experience]. (2nd ed.) Gütersloh, Germany: Bertelsmann, 1930.

This voluminous study has been forgotten even among German psychologists of religion, but unjustly! The work is based on extensive empirical material (the answers given about religious texts such as the *Song of Sun* by Saint Francis of Assisi). Girgensohn extensively describes religious feelings and emotions such as desire or listlessness, worship, exaltation, devotion, anxiety, and fright, but also the processes of will and the different imaginations and intuitions stimulated by religious texts.

Hardy, A. *The Spiritual Nature of Man.* Oxford, England: Clarendon Press, 1979.

This book contains data collected from the first eight years of an ongoing project at the Religious Experience Research Unit, Manchester College, Oxford. The author analyzed about three thousand reported religious experiences by using several categories. His conclusions correspond largely to those of William James (1902): The center of such religious experiences consists of a sense of presence and personalization relative to a higher universe.

Hay, D. *Exploring Inner Space: Scientists and Religious Experience.* London: Mowbray, 1987.

This is essentially a sequel to Hardy's (1979) book.

Hyde, K. E. *Religion in Childhood and Adolescence: A Comprehensive Review of the Research*. Birmingham, Ala.: Religious Education Press, 1991.

Hyde reviews nearly one hundred research reports on religious experience, which is a fraction of the roughly two thousand reports examined in total.

James, W. *The Varieties of Religious Experience*. London: Longmans, Green, 1902.

Although written at the beginning of the century, this book is a classic phenomenological description of religious experience, in general, and of conversion, the experience of the holy, and religious despair, in particular.

Pöll, W. *Das religiöse Erlebnis und seine Strukturen* [The religious experience and its structure]. Munich, Germany: Kösel, 1974.

This book contains chapters about the material structure of religious experience, as well as the functional and personal structure. Additionally, the author considers the religious needs of human beings and the "religious experiences" caused by drugs.

Spilka, B., Hood, R. W., Jr., and Gorsuch, R. L. "Religious Experience." In B. Spilka, R. W. Hood, Jr., and R. L. Gorsuch, *The Psychology of Religion: An Empirical Approach*. Englewood Cliffs, N.J.: Prentice-Hall, 1985.

The authors discuss religious phenomena such as speaking in tongues (glossolalia) and consider extensively the question about the physiological basis of religious experience. Further, the authors present a suggestive research model for religious experiences. In an accompanying chapter (pp. 175-198) the authors deal with mysticism.

Wulff, D. M. *Psychology of Religion: A Study of Classic and Contemporary Views*. New York: Wiley, 1991.

Wulff describes and illustrates ecstatic and mediative states of various religions and cultures, including their ways of attainment in everyday life and in the laboratory.

Conversion

Meadow, M. J., and Kahoe, R. D. "Conversion." In M. J. Meadow and R. D. Kahoe, *Psychology of Religion: Religion in Individual Lives*. New York: Harper & Row, 1984.

These authors also outline the different conversion types, the psychological factors involved, and the effects of conversion (positive benefits).

Paloutzian, R. F. "Conversion Process and Effects." In R. F. Paloutzian, *Invitation to the Psychology of Religion*. Glenview, Ill.: Scott, Foresman, 1983.

In this chapter, Paloutzian discusses three well-known conversion types: sudden, unconscious, and gradual. And he gives phenomenological descriptions and psychological analyses of the conversion itself. Likewise, he considers the effects of this change and its dependence on social groups and factors.

Spilka, B., Hood, R. W., Jr., and Gorsuch, R. L. "Conversion." In B. Spilka, R. W. Hood, Jr., and R. L. Gorsuch, *The Psychology of Religion: An Empirical Approach.* Englewood Cliffs, N.J.: Prentice-Hall, 1985.

The authors also describe the three conversion types considered by Paloutzian (1983). Further, they give an overview of contemporary research on conversion and accentuate the relevance of attributional theory to an explanation of conversion. Especially noteworthy are their explanations of the brainwashing executed in some new religious groups.

Starbuck, E. D. *The Psychology of Religion: An Empirical Study of the Growth of Religious Consciousness.* New York: Walter Scott, 1899.

Based on empirical data presented statistically, the author, a disciple of G. Stanley Hall and William James, deals with conversion as well as religious growth not involving conversion and compares the two lines of religious development.

Religion and Morality

Kohlberg, L., and Power, C. "Moral Development, Religious Thinking, and the Question of a Seventh Stage." In L. Kohlberg, *Essays on Moral Development.* Vol. 1: *The Philosophy of Moral Development.* New York: Harper & Row, 1981.

In this article the authors trace out a seventh stage of moral development, which may be qualified as religious. Further, they consider the relationship between the stages of moral judgment and those of religious development. They conclude that a given stage of moral reasoning is a necessary but not sufficient condition for reaching the corresponding stage of religious judgment.

Meadow, M. J., and Kahoe, R. D. "Altruism and Religious Love." In M. J. Meadow and R. D. Kahoe, *Psychology of Religion: Religion in Individual Lives.* New York: Harper & Row, 1984.

The writers present different types of love (affection, friendship, agape, and so on) and discuss the psychological aspects and dispositions of each. They discuss as well the psychological aspects of the relationship between religiously and morally relevant acts of altruism and charity as stipulated by Jesus in the Sermon on the Mount.

Oser, F., and Reich, K. H. "Moral Judgment, Religious Judgment, World View and Logical Thought. A Review of Their Relationship, Parts 1-2." *British Journal of Religious Education,* 1990, *12,* 94-101, 172-183.

This article contains an overview of different conceptualizations of the relationship between moral and religious development in general and between the corresponding developmental stages. The authors also systematically and empirically compare the stages of moral judgment with those of religious development, including the development of worldviews and logical thought. Finally, they argue for a more dynamic model that takes into account the socialization and experiences of individuals.

Spilka, B., Hood, R. W., Jr., and Gorsuch, R. L. "Religion and Morality." In B. Spilka, R. W. Hood, Jr., and R. L. Gorsuch, *The Psychology of Religion: An Empirical Approach.* Englewood Cliffs, N.J.: Prentice-Hall, 1985.

After general remarks about the relation between religion and morality, the authors deal with concrete moral and ethical problems such as premarital sexual relations, drug use, abuse, and crime. Again, the authors show the relevance of attributional theory to an understanding of such behavior.

Images of God

Bindl, M. F. *Das religiöse Erleben im Spiegel der Bildgestaltung. Eine entwicklungs-psychologische Untersuchung* [The religious experience in the light of subjects' drawings. A developmental psychological study]. Freiburg, Germany: Herder, 1965.

Based on an analysis of 8,205 drawings on religious themes from Roman Catholic students between the ages of three and eighteen, Bindl constructed the existence of four developmental phases: (1) naïve relatedness to the Holy Other, (2) decline in spontaneous experience of the numinous, (3) narcissistic reversion toward self, and (4) consciously striven-for relation to transcendence.

Deconchy, J.-P. "The Idea of God: Its Emergence Between 7 and 16 Years." In A. Godin (ed.), *From Religious Experience to a Religious Attitude.* Brussels: Lumen Vitae Press, 1964.

In his empirical study using the method of associations about the word *God,* the author found three developmental levels of God concepts. First, God is seen as a set of attributes, almost anthropomorphic or animistic in nature; second, (nonphysical) anthropomorphic personalized characteristics predominate (God as friend or father); and, third, the concepts of God are more inward and abstract.

Heller, D. *The Children's God.* Chicago: University of Chicago Press, 1986. The writer extensively interviewed forty children about their representations of the deity. Further, the subjects drew the deity. The findings show that younger children almost dispose of a concrete and anthropomorphistic God-representation, and that socialization by the family must be sufficiently taken into account. For additional analyses of the empirical material, Heller applied psychoanalytic theories, most notably the work of C. G. Jung.

Hutsebout, D. O., and Verhoeven, D. "The Adolescent's Representation of God from Age 12 Until Age 15." In J. M. van der Lans and J. A. van Belzen (eds.), *Proceedings of the Fourth Symposium on the Psychology of Religion in Europe.* Nijmegen, The Netherlands: Department of Cultural Psychology and Psychology of Religion, University of Nijmegen, 1989.

In a longitudinal study of 174 students the authors demonstrate that the development described by Deconchy (1964) in a cross-sectional study was not validated empirically in their study.

Hyde, K. E. *Religion in Childhood and Adolescence: A Comprehensive Review of the Research.* Birmingham, Ala.: Religious Education Press, 1991.

Hyde reviews nearly forty research reports on children's ideas about God, which is a fraction of the roughly two thousand reports examined in total in the volume.

Vergote, A., and Tamayo, A. (eds.). *Parental Figures and the Representation of God: A Psychological and Cross-Cultural Study.* The Hague: Mouton, 1980.

Using especially the semantic-differential as developed by Osgood, the writers investigated the connections of parental figures to God representations among different age groups and within different cultures. They found correspondences between these two categories as well as differences.

Anton A. Bucher is assistant professor at the Pedagogical Institute, University of Fribourg, Fribourg, Switzerland.

K. Helmut Reich is research associate at the Pedagogical Institute, University of Fribourg, Fribourg, Switzerland.

INDEX

ORDERING INFORMATION

NEW DIRECTIONS FOR CHILD DEVELOPMENT is a series of paperback books that presents the latest research findings on all aspects of children's psychological development, including their cognitive, social, moral, and emotional growth. Books in the series are published quarterly in Fall, Winter, Spring, and Summer and are available for purchase by subscription as well as by single copy.

SUBSCRIPTIONS for 1991 cost $48.00 for individuals (a savings of 20 percent over single-copy prices) and $70.00 for institutions, agencies, and libraries. Please do not send institutional checks for personal subscriptions. Standing orders are accepted.

SINGLE COPIES cost $15.95 when payment accompanies order. (California, New Jersey, New York, and Washington, D.C., residents please include appropriate sales tax.) Billed orders will be charged postage and handling.

DISCOUNTS FOR QUANTITY ORDERS are available. Please write to the address below for information.

ALL ORDERS must include either the name of an individual or an official purchase order number. Please submit your order as follows:
    Subscriptions: specify series and year subscription is to begin
    Single copies: include individual title code (such as CD1)

MAIL ALL ORDERS TO:
    Jossey-Bass Inc., Publishers
    350 Sansome Street
    San Francisco, California 94104

FOR SALES OUTSIDE OF THE UNITED STATES CONTACT:
    Maxwell Macmillan International Publishing Group
    866 Third Avenue
    New York, New York 10022

OTHER TITLES AVAILABLE IN THE
NEW DIRECTIONS FOR CHILD DEVELOPMENT SERIES
William Damon, Editor-in-Chief